PILGRIM

PILGRIM

A Theological Memoir

Tony Campolo
with Steve Rabey

WILLIAM B. EERDMANS PUBLISHING COMPANY
GRAND RAPIDS, MICHIGAN

Wm. B. Eerdmans Publishing Co.
4035 Park East Court SE, Grand Rapids, Michigan 49546
www.eerdmans.com

Published 2025

Book design by Lydia Hall

Printed in the United States of America

31 30 29 28 27 26 25 1 2 3 4 5 6 7

ISBN 978-0-8028-8494-7

Library of Congress Cataloging-in-Publication Data

A catalog record for this book is available from the Library of Congress.

CONTENTS

PART 3: HUNGER AND THIRST FOR RIGHTEOUSNESS

PART 4: PUBLIC THEOLOGIAN

PART 5: THE END OF THE ROAD

PART 1

WHEN I WAS A CHILD

CHAPTER 1

ONE PILGRIM'S JOURNEY

For years I toyed with the idea of writing an autobiography, but this remained little more than an idea as long as I continued my time-consuming work of traveling and speaking. I have always imagined myself keeling over behind a pulpit or a podium somewhere. When my work was finally stripped from me by a debilitating stroke that left me partially paralyzed, I finally had more than enough time to take a good look back at the past eighty-eight years of my life.

I call this book a theological memoir because I have focused on events and challenges along the way that forced me to rethink how I conceived and lived out my faith. I began this process as a young person before I had even considered formulating a theology. I am still theologizing today, incorporating new insights into my faith as I reflect on aging, my mortality, and preparing to meet my Maker sometime soon.

This kind of evaluation is something all of us do as we try to answer life's big questions:

Who am I?
Where did I come from?
Why am I here?
What is the meaning of my life?
Where am I going?

I hope this book will not only show you how I navigated this theological journey but also help you reflect on the theological issues you have likely dealt with in your life. I believe every person is a theologian, not only the people who study or teach the subject in books or at seminary.

Each one of us makes decisions and choices about what we believe about God, the Bible, Christ's life, and his teaching. For many, these important decisions happen daily, often below the level of conscious awareness.

And each one of us faces existential life situations that force us to stop, reconsider our assumptions and commitments, and articulate our beliefs in new ways that incorporate what we have learned along the way.

That has certainly been the case with me as I was forced to figure out what I believed about various worldviews and movements that started pressing in on me as a teenager and as a young man, including the civil rights movement, the movement against the war in Vietnam, the sexual revolution, the women's liberation movement, the LGBTQ movement, the pushback against consumerism, and Christian responses to social-justice needs, to name a few.

A Worldly Homebody

I have traveled around the world to speak to churches, professional organizations, and various community groups, worked with Christian leaders and ministries, and supported faith-based aid organizations. Along the way I earned preferred traveler status and racked up untold frequent-flier miles with nearly every major airline.

Meanwhile, I have been a committed homebody who has spent nearly ninety years living and working within a twenty-five-square-mile area around Philadelphia. This familiar and comfortable space is where I was born, and it is probably where

I will die. Here is where I came to faith, married, ministered as a pastor, raised a family, and taught sociology at Eastern University, a Christian university, and at the University of Pennsylvania.

In a similar sense, my decades-long theological journey has exposed me to all manner of discourse, debate, and disagreement. But in the long run, I have continually returned to the bedrock beliefs and values I held when Jesus first entered my heart and gave me his promise of forgiveness, salvation, and eternal life.

I have often been pegged and criticized as being progressive or liberal, and I am fine with being known as the most visible evangelical leader to face a twentieth-century heresy trial, in which I defended myself against false charges about my beliefs.

Some may be surprised to learn that the foundation of my faith experience is a core of fundamentalist beliefs I first learned in our family's Baptist church and later embraced as a member of an on-fire youth organization called the Bible Buzzards, which taught that Christians should shun the sinful world that Jesus died to save.

I eventually left fundamentalism for evangelicalism. I take issue with the recent politicization of evangelicalism in American culture, but it is still the case that evangelicalism remains the best description of my theological home. The evangelicalism that I know is marked by its emphasis on a high view of Scripture, which I believe is an infallible guide for faith and practice; its emphasis on a personal transformative relationship with the resurrected Christ; its adherence to the Apostles' Creed; and its calling to go out into the world and share the love of Jesus with others.

Over the decades, no matter which theological, philosophic, moral, or ethical conundrum I was trying to figure out, I have always relied on this fairly simple spiritual toolbox to guide my thinking.

A Pilgrim Seeking My Eternal Home

I have enjoyed a great life that has allowed me to pursue my intellectual and theological passions, brought me unexpected celebrity as a speaker and major media appearances, and allowed me to serve as a counselor to the president of the United States. Not bad for a driven boy who came from humble, immigrant-family origins. But as comfortable as life has been for me in this world, I have always known that my brief sojourn here is only a prelude to something even better: eternal life in a newly resurrected and perfected body, and in a new heaven and new earth prepared for us by God (Rev. 21:1). I have long set my sights on that new world.

My life has been a search for something the Christian activist William Stringfellow described in the title of one of his books: *An Ethic for Christians and Other Aliens in a Strange Land*. I have done the best I could in fulfilling the calling God gave me. Now I await my next assignment.

CHAPTER 2

FAITH OF OUR FATHERS (AND MOTHERS)

On February 25, 1935, I was born into a struggling Italian immigrant family of four living in South Philadelphia. In the beginning, I came to my faith the way most kids do. I inherited my beliefs about God and life from my parents. In my family, as it happened, my parents looked at the world from differing perspectives throughout their lives.

Anthony Campolo Sr. was a good, loving, quiet man who landed in Philadelphia as a penniless teenager after an earthquake and tsunami hit his hometown of Messina in Sicily, killing his parents and destroying much of the city. His older brother had come to America first to test things out, and once he had established himself, my dad followed. My father's life here was better than it would have been back home, but he struggled all his life with the English language and never really mastered it. From the day he landed, he worked hard at a series of low-paying jobs until his body finally gave out.

Work was initially hard to find in Philadelphia, so my dad made his way to Canada and found employment with the Canadian Expeditionary Force, which sent him to France to fight in the trenches for nearly the entire duration of World War I.

Exposure to German mustard gas, along with injuries and illnesses, affected his service and would later cut short his life. He was sent to a hospital in England, where he met a nurse who promised to write him letters and later join him in America so they could be married. But his sister back in Philadelphia disapproved, and after my father returned from the war and moved into his sister's home, she secretly intercepted and destroyed the letters before they could reach my father. He was left to wonder what happened to the English nurse he had hoped to marry.

Mary Piccirilli was born to a teenage bride who had arrived at Ellis Island from a small town in southern Italy and had married another poor Italian immigrant in Philadelphia. Mary was just nine years old when her father died, leaving his young widow and their several children destitute, hungry, and cold. Mary and her siblings almost wound up in an orphanage, but assistance from an Italian Baptist church enabled the family to stay intact. Mary's mother remarried, and more children followed. Mary was a smart girl and a quick learner, but her stepfather got her a cleaning job in a downtown jewelry store at the age of eleven so she could help support the family, and she had to drop out of school. That was the way things were in Italian immigrant families.

The differences between my mother and father were a constant source of amazement and amusement, and on occasion a source of conflict. Mom was a powerful personality who loved to talk. She often drowned out Dad's occasional attempts at conversation, and she gave her gift of gab to me and my two older sisters. Together, the four extroverted members of the family enjoyed dinners overflowing with wide-ranging discussions, intense debates, and raucous laughter. Meanwhile, Dad sat silently at his end of the dinner table, the high-decibel verbal onslaught surrounding him with little apparent effect.

One Home, Two Value Systems

In addition to their dramatic personality differences, Mom and Dad also embraced differing views on faith and politics. They had both been raised Catholic. Mom wound up rejecting Catholicism and joining a Baptist church. Even as a girl, she thoroughly adopted the fundamentalist teaching that prevailed at the time, which was decades before people started talking about a new movement called evangelicalism. Dad joined the same Baptist church when he returned to Philadelphia after his wartime service, and it was there that he met and married my mom. Even so, he never totally abandoned some of his deep-seated Catholic devotional practices, such as his respect for saints.

Politics was another topic on which my parents had conflicting loyalties. Mom's fundamentalist faith squared entirely with her Republican Party loyalties and her suspicions about the "socialism" of Franklin D. Roosevelt, who was first elected president in 1932 during the depths of the Depression and re-elected three times.

Dad was a diehard Democrat who loved FDR, and a loyal union man who fought for greater economic equality for workers. The many social programs FDR instituted were a lifeline for poor, struggling laborers like my dad, who felt like a perpetual underdog in a world run by money and power. He would often bring home union brochures and other literature.

I was only a year old in 1936 when FDR ran for a second term, so I knew nothing about that election. I followed the action a little bit in 1940. By the time I was nine years old in 1944, I was ready to make my own choice of who should be elected.

We followed the party conventions that year on the radio, and when I heard FDR's incumbent vice president, Henry A. Wallace, make his speech, I was sold. Wallace was a liberal idealist who described the twentieth century as "the century of the common man." Although Harry S. Truman ultimately beat Wallace for the nomination for vice president in 1944, I became a Democrat on the day I heard Wallace share his progressive vision on the convention floor, and I have remained one ever since.

"True Christians"

I can hardly remember a time when our family was not in church while I was growing up. The Campolos were pillars of the congregation at New Berean Baptist Church, which stood at the corner of 59th and Pine Streets. We were present at church every Sunday—for Sunday school, the morning worship service, and the evening service—and every Wednesday for the evening prayer meeting.

We were proud to be fundamentalists. We were taught that if you were not a fundamentalist, you were not a true Christian. We felt that certain Catholics were not true Christians, which caused tensions within our extended Italian-Catholic families. Even Episcopalians were suspect. "They're just Catholics who don't know how to read and write in Latin," one church elder told me.

At New Berean, we heard a few basic doctrines hammered home over and over: God created the world, humankind sinned, and Jesus came to save us from sin. Everything we believed came straight from the Bible, which we understood was verbally inspired by God and completely inerrant. I pictured God whispering words into the apostle Paul's ear, and Paul copying down everything, just as God told him. We were never allowed to question anything in the Bible, no matter how strange it might seem. Even so, some Bible verses posed real challenges to our commitment to literal interpretation, such as 1 Samuel 18:27: "David took his men with him and went out and killed two hundred Philistines and brought back their foreskins."

Two popular slogans accurately summed up our faith. The first slogan: "We don't smoke, we don't chew, and we don't dance with girls that do." We pursued holiness through negation: no movies, no loose or promiscuous behavior, and no drinking, even at Sunday Communion. Catholics used wine in the Mass, but we used watered-down grape juice.

Once in a while I would hear at church about a family that had a glass of wine with dinner, but that was generally kept quiet to avoid controversy. Our teetotaling ways did not make any sense to our Catholic relatives. My Uncle Tom, a Catholic, thought our teetotalism was ridiculous and non-Christian.

"So, what about the miracle when Jesus turned water into wine?" he asked. "Are you saying Jesus just turned the water into grape juice?"

The second slogan was based on the classic hymn "On Christ the Solid Rock I Stand," which features this memorable chorus: "My hope is built on nothing less than Jesus' blood and righteousness." We revised that chorus to this: "My hope is built on nothing less than Scofield notes and Scripture Press." This referred to the interpretive notes in the Scofield Reference Bible, and the Sunday-school curriculum published by Scripture Press near Chicago.

Fundies, but Not Fighters

We were "fundies" through and through, but I thank God to this day that we were not "flamin', fightin' fundies" like the antagonistic believers who continuously railed about communism, Charles Darwin, Hollywood movies, and other sinister influences. Some fundamentalist churches were—and are—so toxic and hate-filled that their fear and anger overpowered their commitment to the love of Christ.

At New Berean, we knew the world was sinful, but we did not see everyone outside the church walls as our enemy. We believed what Jesus taught, so we tried to love our neighbors, even if they were living in sin.

I can still remember a sermon illustration our pastor used that made holiness clear to me. Back in 1927, Charles Lindbergh completed the first solo, nonstop transatlantic flight in his airplane, the *Spirit of St. Louis*. The young pilot was a worldwide hero, so our pastor, a no-nonsense former army chaplain, hitched his sermon to Lindbergh's death-defying flight.

As he told us, Lindbergh was flying alone over the Atlantic Ocean when he realized there was a stowaway in the fuselage. A rat had hidden on the plane and was now busily chewing on anything he could find: Lindbergh's limited food rations, a glove, and the rubber fuel line that powered the plane.

The primitive plane did not have autopilot, so he could not leave his seat to trap the rodent. But if the rat kept munching away, the plane could plummet into the sea. What could Lindbergh do? He could guide his plane higher and higher, until he reached such an altitude that the rat would pass out from lack of oxygen.

"When Satan attacks, you win victory over sin by flying higher," the pastor said. "The higher you go, the more life's problems will fall away."

It made perfect sense. The closer you are to God, the higher you rise in your Christian life, and the less temptation and sin will bring you back down to sinful earth. Some fundamentalists talked about fighting this evil world. Sometimes, we preferred to flee it.

Born Again, and Again, and Again

Altar calls and invitations to receive Christ as Savior were normal fare at New Berean, and over the years, my anxieties about the status of my salvation led me to respond to these pleas more than once. I got to know what it felt like to walk down the aisle. One of the first times I accepted Christ was at a huge crusade featuring Hyman Jedidiah Appelman, a Russian-born Jewish convert to Christianity who evangelized around the world from the 1930s to the 1970s. He was a Baptist Billy Graham before Billy Graham.

In 1942, more than two hundred churches brought Appelman to Philadelphia for a three-week crusade that started out at Town Hall (a beautiful building that no longer exists) and then moved to Convention Hall when the crowds grew larger. Mine was one of five thousand decisions for Christ that Appelman recorded during his time there.

After the service, I was taken backstage to learn what it meant to accept Jesus in my heart. I learned that God the Father is in heaven, but Jesus, his Son, is down here with us and is living inside me now that I have accepted him as my Savior. It seemed simple enough, but on some nights I would lie awake wondering if I was a true Christian, and if I had a real relationship with Christ.

Communion Miracle

Revival meetings were more exciting than the regular services at New Berean Baptist, but I loved my church, which was part of the American Baptist denomination. I would remain a part of this denomination for the rest of my life, and I went to school and taught at a denominational college.

Even my dad got into the swing of things and gradually adapted to life as a Baptist. But his reverence for Catholicism remained, especially for the ritual of Mass, as he revealed one Sunday morning at New Berean. It was the monthly Communion Sunday, and our pastor preached a tough sermon on this tough verse: "So then, whoever eats the bread or drinks the cup of the Lord in an unworthy manner will be guilty of sinning against the body and blood of the Lord. Everyone ought to examine themselves before they eat of the bread and drink from the cup" (1 Cor. 11:27–28).

The sermon moved many people, including the woman sitting alone in the pew in front of our family. As the sermon progressed, we could see her wiping away tears. By the end she was crying openly as she worried about taking Communion unworthily.

As the elders started passing plates of bread through the pews, my dad worried that this young woman was about to deny herself this vital sacrament. Before the bread arrived at her pew, my normally silent, introverted father did something I never saw him do before or since.

He leaned forward, placed his hand gently on the woman's shoulder, and said something to her in a quiet, firm voice. We could hear him clearly.

"Take it, girl. It was meant for you. Take it."

That was the closest thing to a miracle I had seen thus far.

Double Discipleship

When I was not at church, or at revival meetings, God continued to work his ways in my life through two trusty assistants: my older sisters Rose and Ann. In a sense, I was raised by three mothers. The sermons and Sunday-school lessons I heard at church were reinforced by Rose and Ann, two of the kindliest spiritual mentors I have ever known.

But life was not all lessons on sin and salvation. My sisters were fun, and they loved taking me to exciting events like the annual Thanksgiving Day Parade in Philadelphia. Our parade—which was sponsored by the Gimbel Brothers department store and began years before Macy's New York City parade—could attract half a million people in good years. And at Christmas, they would take me downtown to Gimbels, so I could see Santa and ask him for the electric train set I pined for, year after year.

All in all, I enjoyed a good, calm life. But the calm would be disrupted once I began to seek my own ways of growing my simple faith in Jesus.

CHAPTER 3

ME AGAINST THE WORLD

In addition to our three weekly services at New Berean Baptist Church, Mom made sure we practiced our faith at home, with family prayer being a regular mealtime ritual. And in the summer we kids went to Bible camp. You would think this steady diet of religious instruction would be enough to keep me satisfied, but starting in the eighth grade and continuing for the next five years, I would also devote every Saturday evening to faith and fellowship, joining a group that offered Christian meetings tailored specifically to young people.

The group was not Youth for Christ, the national youth movement that began during the 1940s and would sweep the nation, thanks in part to its popular new evangelist, a young man named Billy Graham. Instead, I joined a small, homegrown Philadelphia group of dozens of young souls that had an unlikely name: the Bible Buzzards.

I loved the group for its energy, its rigorous study of Scripture, and its tight-knit community. What I did not initially realize is that this group embraced a hardcore fundamentalist theology that differed from what I learned at New Berean. Before long, these theological differences would cause my first-ever crisis of faith.

Feasting on God's Word

It all began at William C. Bryant Elementary School, located at 60th Street and Cedar Avenue in Philadelphia. It was at Bryant that I first met Burton Neumann, who would become a lifelong best friend and Christian companion. One day after recess at Bryant, Burt began talking to me about Christ. Realizing that he was trying to evangelize me, I let him know I was already a Christian. He was relieved, and the two of us became fast friends.

Later, Burt invited me to accompany him to a Saturday evening meeting of the youth group. I was interested in going, but was confused about the group's name.

"What's a Bible Buzzard?" I asked.

"Well," Burt explained, "you know how vultures feast on bodies of dead animals? We feed on the living Word of God."

And sure enough, every Saturday night, thirty to sixty young people would meet at one of the members' homes for an evening of fun, fellowship, powerful singing, and line-by-line study of New Testament books. We met twice at my family's tiny little rowhouse home, and those meetings were incredibly cramped, with some Buzzards having no choice but to squeeze in under the dining-room table.

After arriving for each meeting, each of us would settle into a spot on the floor or the stairs, and then the enthusiastic singing would start. It lasted for about forty-five minutes and was usually loud enough to be heard by nearby neighbors. Because I could hold a tune and had attended a Billy Graham crusade, I became the weekly song leader. I loved leading our group in singing classic revival hymns like "The Wonderful Grace of Jesus" and "When the Roll Is Called Up Yonder," all sung in tight four-part harmonies. I still love those old hymns much more than contemporary songs.

We would typically spend a good half hour or more in intense Bible study followed by another twenty to thirty minutes in prayer. Then, after a few hours together, we would rush off to Howard Johnson's or some other local restaurant to hang out, eat pie and ice cream, and talk for another hour or two.

There was much to love about the Buzzards. Our leader, a Bible-studying accountant named Tom Roop, was as devoted to in-depth Bible study as he was to personally ministering to his young disciples. Many of us would spend long evenings at his house, pouring out our hearts about various issues in our lives, and likely driving Tom's long-suffering wife, Mabel, nuts.

As I would learn later when I studied sociology, the Bible Buzzards provided us young disciples with a "plausibility structure" that made our faith more real and relatable. When I attended New Berean, I felt I was inheriting a faith that belonged to my parents. Among the Buzzards, faith was ours to claim and live out. The group reinforced and sustained me in my Christian commitment.

Many of us Buzzards lived out our faith thoroughly, and in addition to our Saturday-evening meetings and weekly services at our respective churches, the most devoted among us also organized Friday-night street meetings, where we would present the gospel on busy street corners and in parks. We accompanied ourselves with music, depending on who showed up. Sometimes a lone trumpet announced our presence. Other nights it was our gospel quartet, the Sword of the Lord.

On occasion, we would work with local Youth for Christ groups to stage more elaborate outreaches. These rallies, usually on Thursday and Friday nights, were held at a town hall we rented for the occasion.

During my high-school years, the Buzzards put together a kind of traveling road show that would visit local churches on Sunday mornings, sing, offer a brief message, and challenge young people to follow Christ. And during the summers, we ran our own Bible conference at the YMCA's Camp Ockanickon in New Jersey, combining fun, Christian teaching, and many repetitions of the popular song "Kumbaya."

These varied evangelistic efforts taught me two things that became building blocks of my later speaking career. First, you need to project your voice, or nobody will hear you. Second, you need good stories so that those who hear you become interested in what you have to say.

Tom Roop taught us that Christianity is more than a spectator sport. It was a living faith we must embrace with our whole lives. This commitment led dozens of young Buzzards to become pastors and missionaries. For the rest of my life, winning souls for Christ would be a major part of my mission. I would not have gone into ministry had it not been for Tom Roop.

God Loves the World, but We Should Not

There was much to love about the Bible Buzzards, but not everything I heard on Saturday nights fit in with what I heard at New Berean on Sunday mornings. Long before I ever knew what theology is, or what fundamentalism means, the Buzzards forced me to wrestle with conflicting teachings about sin, holiness, and how Christians should interact with the world.

The main difference between my two faith communities was that the Bible Buzzards were much more fearful of "the world" than the believers at New Berean. At New Berean, I learned that all people sin and fall short of God's glory, but God loved the world so much that he sent his Son to save us. Christians who have been redeemed and restored now have a duty to reach out to the world, both spiritually (by praying for and evangelizing sinners) and socially (by working for the improvement of social conditions until God's kingdom comes in its fullness).

The Bible Buzzards agreed that people sin (mostly non-Christians) and that these sinners need to hear God's saving message. But Tom Roop insisted that, except for venturing out to witness and preach to others, Christians should stay far away from the world and all its temptations. One of Tom's favorite verses from his big, thoroughly underlined Scofield Reference version of the King James Bible emphasized this point: "And what agreement hath the temple of God with idols? for ye are the temple of the living God; as God hath said, I will dwell in them, and walk in them; and I will be their God, and they shall be my people. Wherefore come out from among them, and be ye separate, saith the Lord, and touch not the unclean thing; and I will receive you" (2 Cor. 6:16–17).

Years later, when I would learn the meanings of all kinds of complex theological words, I would realize that the Bible Buzzards' theology was a mixture of two things: fundamentalist pietism and dispensational eschatology.

To the Buzzards, these verses meant that we should flee the world and its many powerful temptations and focus instead on prayer and spiritual purity, as the world is a dirty and dangerous place that will get worse and worse until Jesus comes back and the world ends in a massive apocalypse. This was the opposite of what I heard at New Berean, which taught that Christians should go out and work in the world to make it better for everyone, even though it is still dominated by sin.

I had no idea how all these intellectual and theological tensions would work themselves out, but the situation did not bother me too much until it threatened to undo my senior year of high school.

A Dance with the Devil?

At school, I followed my mom's example, not my dad's. I blossomed into an extroverted student who used all my social connections to win election as student-body president at West Philadelphia High School.

There was just one problem. As student-body president, it was my duty to help organize our senior prom. But the prom was a big dance. Tweaking lyrics from the song, "Ya Got Trouble," from the popular Broadway musical *The Music Man*, you could say:

You got trouble, folks, right here in Philly City,
trouble with a capital "T"
And that rhymes with "D" and that stands for dance.

My parents and the members of New Berean were proud that a good Christian boy like me had become his high school's student president. My sister Rose taught me the latest dance styles. We practiced dancing in the basement while playing hit songs by Frank Sinatra and other pop stars on our primitive little phonograph.

But to my friends in the Bible Buzzards, my role as a prom promoter was a serious violation of the group's moral code. Tom Roop had always taught that dancing was sinful, and not only would I be presiding over a sinful dance, but I had also invited another Bible Buzzard to be my date.

Tom spelled out my many offenses against God and man. First, my role in organizing and promoting the prom not only exposed me to unnecessary temptation. I was also encouraging others to engage in sin, thereby harming my witness for Christ and the reputation of all my Bible Buzzards friends. Plus, not only was I jeopardizing my salvation, but by inviting a fellow Buzzard to be my partner for the evening, I was leading a dedicated Christian young woman away from the Lord and jeopardizing her salvation too.

The stakes were very high. As Tom asked me, "If you two go to the prom, will anybody ever take us seriously again when we talk about living a holy life?"

In Praise of Guardrails

In my heart, I knew that Tom and the Buzzards were wrong. And all in all, the prom was a wonderful event, even if my joy was dimmed by unnecessary clouds of guilt and doubt. I was not kicked out of the Buzzards, but I had violated one of the group's sacred norms, and I would pay by losing my privileged standing with Tom and other members. I still played an active role in their weekly meetings and regular outreach events, but I was no longer Tom's golden boy, and our relationship now felt strained.

These tensions caused me much turmoil and eventually led me to walk away from fundamentalism. Even so, I want to say a few words in its defense as a means of protecting young people from the potentially damaging sins of youth. Years after my fateful prom, I began working more closely with college students. Time after time, I talked with young men and women whose lives had been upended by destructive sexual entanglements. The Bible Buzzards—who taught that if you cannot end a date with prayer, you are dating the wrong person—helped me keep my raging teenage hormones in check. I am not alone. Fundamentalism has helped millions of young people avoid a lot of trouble, and for that I am grateful.

The conservative focus of the Bible Buzzards also cemented my commitment to Christ, my belief that evangelism is a core part of the Christian mission, and my choice to serve Christ with my life and vocational choices, first as a pastor and later as a teacher, author, and speaker.

On the other hand, I regret that I got so totally sucked into Tom Roop's dispensationalist fundamentalist theology. For years, it made me a sin-obsessed, judgmental kid who would harass nearly everyone I met, asking if they were saved or were going to hell.

Only much later, after years of Christian college and seminary, would I learn to shake off the most destructive aspects of this theology, and even then, it was only with great difficulty that I managed to do so.

CHAPTER 4

ARE MY JEWISH FRIENDS REALLY GOING TO HELL?

For years, South Philly—which would later become famous as the setting for *Rocky*—was a great neighborhood for our struggling family of Italian-American strivers. By the time I was born, however, my dad had moved the family several miles away, to a Delancey Street rowhouse in a West Philadelphia neighborhood that was largely Jewish. Our family took firm root in West Philadelphia, and that is where I grew up.

My poorly educated dad wanted to make sure that his only son took school seriously and got a good education. He believed that my growing up with Jewish friends might provide me with more academic encouragement than I was likely to find on the streets of South Philly. Certainly, the location of our home in West Philadelphia made my dad's long workdays even harder, by lengthening the commute, by bus and on foot, to his job at the RCA manufacturing plant in Camden, New Jersey.

West Philadelphia was a fun neighborhood for a kid like me. For one thing, the neighborhood was home to TV station WFIL (now WPVI), where a popular local show called *American Bandstand* was starting to attract audiences beyond Philadelphia.

Kids would rush to the studio and line up outside, eager to dance on the show and be television stars for a few moments. But some of the tougher kids from school would make fun of these dancers and mess up the guys' slicked-back pompadours.

As I grew taller, I jumped at the opportunity to play for New Berean Baptist Church's newly formed basketball team. We struggled to find enough players to field a full team, so I asked some of my Jewish friends if they wanted to join my church team. Through an interesting episode of interfaith dialogue, the church elders came up with a satisfactory plan for allowing this to happen. My Jewish teammates did not need to convert to Christianity, but they were required to attend our church youth-group meetings on Sunday nights.

Everything worked out pretty well. I was doing my homework, earning good grades, and even winning the occasional award for academic achievement, just like Dad had hoped. My Jewish friends were much more serious about school than my Italian friends were, just as Dad had predicted. My Italian friends would skip school just to hang out and have fun, but when my Jewish friends skipped school, they were likely to do something like taking in a Shakespeare movie festival. I can still remember watching Laurence Olivier play the role of Hamlet on the silver screen on one occasion when we played hooky.

The more I got to know and love these amazing Jewish boys and gain more understanding of their faith and ancient traditions, the more I felt we were all following the same God somehow. Could my Jewish friends follow God without following Christ?

While some members of New Berean quietly prayed that these nice Jewish boys would accept Christ, others loudly claimed that salvation came only through Christ, and that if Jews did not accept Christ as their Savior, they would burn in hell for all eternity. Trying to figure this out would lead to my next major theological challenge.

Hoop Dreams

Philadelphia was crazy for basketball, even before the Philadelphia Warriors (who are now the Golden State Warriors) won the national championship in 1947 behind the shooting of "Jumping Joe" Fulks, who regularly broke scoring records and once scored sixty-three points in a single game.

For reasons I cannot explain, many professional basketball players would come from our little neighborhood, but I knew next to nothing about the game until I found myself on my church's team. I had never played before, and no one had ever tried to teach me. I needed to learn quickly to help our church team, so I walked a mile and a half to a public park where the Black kids played, sat down, and watched every move they made. When they took a break, I grabbed the ball and tried my best to copy what they had done. In both skill and skin tone, my playing was a pale imitation. Even so, I practiced long and hard enough to land a starting position on New Berean's basketball team.

We recruited others with evangelical zeal. With the West Philadelphia Jewish Center a half mile to the west, and St. Carthage Catholic Church about a mile away in the opposite direction, we came up with a team roster that featured me and a handful of fellow Baptists, seven Jews, and two Catholics.

The presence of Catholics on the team infuriated some of the New Berean fundamentalists even more than the presence of Jewish players because these fundamentalists believed that the Catholic Church was not really Christian, and even anti-Christian. Even worse, it was led by the pope, whom they considered the Antichrist. Such attitudes inspired virulent—and sometimes violent—repression and discrimination against Catholics, simply because they were Catholics.

My Catholic teammates regularly asked me about Baptists, including questions about who was the "head" of the church. It took me a while to figure out what they were asking, but I learned to confidently tell them, "Baptists don't have a pope."

Team members would sit together during Sunday-night youth services at New Berean, which had a nice gym in the basement. We played our games on Monday and Thursday nights, except for one unforgettable Friday night when we played a brief exhibition game during the halftime of a Warriors game. What a thrill!

We played other church teams, including those from the Fourth Presbyterian Church and the Bethany Presbyterian Church, which John Wanamaker had helped to found (and which had the best gym of all the churches). We also played the team from the nearby Orthodox church, which had some big, heavy guys who would push us around quite a bit. I remember getting pretty banged up in our games against that team.

I would soon get to know the Jewish and Catholic players on our team much better, and during the next few years, I would come to love them all. That only made me feel worse about the possibility that they might all be on their way to hell, unless some caring Christian like me presented the gospel to them and saved them from certain eternal damnation.

"You Shall Be My People"

At the Bible Buzzards meetings, we mostly studied books of the New Testament, but at New Berean, we would often hear Old Testament lessons from Genesis, the Psalms, Proverbs, or one of the prophets. I was also reading through the Old Testament by myself during my devotional time. Having seven close Jewish friends somehow made the Old Testament come alive for me in a new way. As I read, I felt I was learning about their faith, just as they learned about my faith when they came to church on Sunday nights.

As I read, I came across one reference—and then many—that testified to God's enduring love for the Jewish people. The prophet Jeremiah states it most clearly: "So you will be my people, and I will be your God" (30:22). I soon realized that similar wording appears two dozen times in the "Jewish" parts of the Bible.

As far as I could see, my Jewish and Catholic teammates believed in the same biblical God I believed in. They were good boys with strict morals. They were not evil, and it troubled me to picture them burning in hell when they were often more honest and faithful than I was, which was embarrassing for a Baptist!

Once again, life was forcing me to wrestle with questions that confused me. This was still years before I finally realized there was a powerful tool called theology that I could use to navigate my way out of such jams.

After World War II ended and the horrors of the Holocaust were widely revealed, theologians began asking if Christians' insensitive rhetoric about Jews had helped bring about widespread public acceptance of Hitler's final solution.

Years later, when I was a student at Eastern Baptist College (now Eastern University) in St. Davids, Pennsylvania, I first heard of something called covenant theology, which is also known as "two covenant" or "dual covenant" theology. The concept is that Jews and Gentiles are covered by two different covenants, and that Jews who believe in God are not required to come to faith in Christ. Understandably, this is a delicate issue, and some theologians argue that any dual covenant denies the centrality of Christ's work on the cross.

After I encountered covenant theology, I felt as if I finally had an answer to some of the questions about Christians and Jews that I had been trying to figure out since my days on the New Berean basketball team.

CHAPTER 5

BUSILY DOING TWO KINDS OF WORK

Sociologists around the world are familiar with the Protestant work ethic, Max Weber's concept that Christian faith can encourage characteristics such as diligence, discipline, and frugality that promote prosperity and strengthen capitalism. I have long admired Weber's work, but it does not deal with one important driver of success that I know about from personal experience: the impoverished Italian-American immigrant work ethic.

Like so many of Philadelphia's Italian-American families, ours struggled to survive on my father's low wages. He worked hard, but he lacked skills, and he could not speak English very well. He never made more than fifty dollars a week, which was not much for a family of five. Not everyone in the extended family thought he worked hard enough, and some of our relatives suggested he was too passive, and that if he really cared for his family's welfare, he would simply push himself a bit harder to get a job that paid more.

Children growing up in poor immigrant families like mine were expected to do everything they could to contribute to the family's survival and finances and to avoid doing things that would add to the expense burden. For me, this meant work, work, work, from the time I was eight or nine years old. It also meant helping to provide food. Most afternoons I would walk to a nearby park, grab a big clump of the dandelions that seemed to grow everywhere, and bring home the weed's green leaves for our evening salad.

It also meant being satisfied with subpar Christmas presents. I remember one year when I was about five or six years old, Santa brought me a shiny red truck. I played with it for a few months, then forgot about it. Then the next Christmas, I received a shiny blue truck. I played with that one for a few months too. The next Christmas, my present was a shiny yellow truck. That's when I realized my sisters' ploy. Each year, they painted the forgotten truck a new color so I would have a nice present to open on Christmas Day.

We hoped that I would be the first to go to college, but my family had made it clear: there was no money for tuition, so I would have to pay for college myself. So, every time I got paid for one of my many little jobs, I would go home and give half the money to my mom and put the other half in the bank for college. My contributions to the family budget paled in comparison to those of my sisters, both of whom landed good jobs with the Pennsylvania Railroad. Since they were women, and not expected to attend college, they turned over all of their weekly checks to Mom.

I was committed to working as much and as hard as I could, but at the Bible Buzzards I was hearing more Bible lessons about how Christians must also do work for God. It seemed that the more serious you were as a Christian, the more likely it was that you would be a pastor, or even better, a missionary. This was the kind of work that serious believers did, and I dove into this kind of work, too, hoping to further burnish my reputation as a strong Christian believer.

Daily Duties

During the school year, my first duty was to get dressed and go to school. It was after school that my life as a working stiff began, and my main tool was my trusty bicycle, to which I could attach a small trailer. Some afternoons I would ride to the local grocery store and offer to transport people's groceries to their front steps—a valuable service at a time when most people in our neighborhood still made do without automobiles.

On other afternoons, I would head to the local pharmacy, which paid me to deliver prescription medicines to customers. Some of the money I earned from the pharmacy first enabled me to purchase my own bike.

On many days at around 4 p.m., I would ride over to Bond Bread, the big local bakery at 56th and Market Streets. That's when the men who drove the Bond Bread delivery trucks would return from their rounds, often with unsold loaves of bread. I paid the bakery a nickel for each leftover loaf, loaded them in my little trailer, and then rode as fast as I could to three or four local restaurants where I could sell the bread for twenty-five cents a loaf—a 400 percent profit.

Miracle on Market Street

Many days, I did not get home from my rounds until 6 p.m. or later. One freezing night, I got home much later than that. It had been a great day for my bread business, but I was not done yet, though I was dead tired. I was battling a light drizzle that had soaked through my threadbare coat. The moment the sun went down, everything turned to ice, including the pavement and my wet clothes. I remember shivering so severely that I struggled to keep control of my handlebars.

As my bike skidded this way and that over the uneven pavement, I heard a sudden boom. My front tire had blown out and instantly gone flat. I pulled my bike and trailer over to the side of the road, sat on the curb, and began crying hot tears of anger, fear, and frustration. I shouted out my feelings to God in an impromptu prayer: "God, people talk about how you are so wonderful, but I'm not sure you're all that wonderful, or you wouldn't be letting this happen to me right now! So, if you are wonderful, like the Bible and people say you are, please help me out of this mess."

I wiped away my tears, stood up, and began slow-walking my bike and trailer toward home, my front tire flip-flopping on the pavement all the way. I did not think the local gas station would still be open this late, but it was, so I headed toward the tire pump, even though I knew my tire leaked like a sieve.

I attached the hose to my tire, pushed the button to start the flow of pressurized air, and prepared myself for the inevitable disappointment. But to my complete amazement, the tire slowly inflated. Even when I put pressure on it, the tire still held.

I unhooked the air hose and cautiously started pedaling. Before I knew it, I had finished my remaining bread deliveries and made it safely home. I was frozen and partially numb, but grateful.

I did what I always did, ever since my previous bike had been stolen. I put the bike on our little front porch, chained it to a solid wooden porch post, and locked it securely in place. At that moment, I heard a whoosh as all the air in the tire rushed out once again.

That was the first time I ever felt I had seen a real live miracle, even though I had been hearing about miracles at church and reading about them in the Bible for years. Suddenly, I felt as if my little life had been caught up in a modern-day miracle when God supernaturally intervened in his universe. I still consider it a miracle to this day.

Sweating It Out All Summer

During the school year, I squeezed in work around my classes, homework, church, Bible Buzzards, and basketball games. But during the summers, I could work morning, noon, and night making as much money as I could. My days actually started at night. I rode my bike down to the Abbotts Dairy plant, to arrive at 10 p.m. I went to work in a big, cold room where ice cream and popsicles were made. You never knew which until you got there and could tell by the smell whether it was ice cream or one of the juice flavors.

Henry Ford mass-produced cars. We mass-produced frozen treats. There was one big, long vat full of liquid and hundreds of little lead containers that traveled around the room on a conveyor belt. One big machine filled the containers with liquid. The next big machine inserted wooden sticks into a hundred containers at a time. Then they headed for the freezer unit for quick cooldown.

As soon as they came out of the freezer, it was my job to stand there, grab the containers, and pry out the popsicles. I did that for hours on end, night after night, which contributed to the arthritis I have had in my thumbs for years. Plus, unlimited access to confections meant I gained weight.

Working in a room full of machines, I always wondered why they could not come up with a machine to take care of that final step. They eventually did. When I visited the dairy years later, machines were now doing my old job.

I would wrap up at the dairy by 8 a.m. and some days I would then head off to a local plastic factory, where I would spend eight hours a day making my cold thumbs very hot. The factory made dials for radios. I would fill small, round molds with plastic powder, which would then be superheated, emerging as a plastic solid, which I had to remove from the mold with my thumbs.

And still, my summer workday was not done. After my shift at the plastic factory, it was time to become a Good Humor man. I would dress up in the white uniform, hop on a company-owned bike, and ride through different neighborhoods in the afternoon, ringing my bell and calling out the names of delicious frozen treats to all of the children within earshot.

After a busy summer of hard work, I was always ready to return to the slower pace of the school year. But I never forgot what it was like to work hard for little pay and to subject my body to regular abuse along the way. My dad had always sung the praise of hardworking Americans, and now I knew what he meant.

At times, I earned as much or more than my dad earned in a given week. I had mixed feelings about that. I was proud to be doing my manly duty in my family, and my mother praised me for my diligence. But I was sad that adults like my father made as little as they did at their low-paying blue-collar jobs. This experience gave me an undying compassion for the plight of people at the lower end of America's socioeconomic scale. Some people insist that with enough will and determination, anyone can pull himself up by his bootstraps. But what about those who do not even have boots?

My Other Work

I was a busy boy, but as I learned when I went to Bible Buzzards, there was an additional kind of work I needed to do. I must work for God. Tom Roop repeatedly taught on Christ's Great Commission: "Therefore go and make disciples of all nations, baptizing them in the name of the Father and of the Son and of the Holy Spirit, and teaching them to obey everything I have commanded you. And surely I am with you always, to the very end of the age" (Matt. 28:19–20).

I was not sure what kind of work I wanted to do for God, but it seemed that there were two options: to become a pastor or to become a missionary. Our pastor at New Berean Baptist Church had served as an army chaplain, and I thought that sounded interesting. But Tom made it clear that the highest work of all was service as a missionary in faraway places, such as deepest Africa. That's what the super-Christians did.

I wanted to be a super-Christian, so I started thinking about where I might be a missionary someday, but I was not entirely sure that was for me. In the meantime, my Bible Buzzard friends and I continued our street-corner preaching, Sunday church talks, and summer camps, giving all of us practical experience in ministry.

CHAPTER 6

A WOULD-BE JUNIOR GALILEO

I loved to watch Flash Gordon on the grainy screen of our little black-and-white TV every Saturday. One movie serial, called *Space Soldiers*, was pretty good. But *Space Soldiers Conquer the Universe* was even better. A deadly plague called the Purple Death was being spread around the world by a group of antagonistic space aliens. The fatal illness left a telltale purple mark on victims' foreheads. Flash Gordon and his pals traveled all the way to the planet Mongo, where they convinced Ming the Merciless to stop spreading the plague.

But *Flash Gordon's Trip to Mars* was my favorite Flash Gordon movie serial. In this one, a powerful but mysterious beam of light from outer space was being aimed at Earth, wreaking havoc on our atmosphere. Flash and his gang took off for the source of the problem, suspecting that the bad dudes on planet Mongo were, once again, to blame. But as it turned out, Ming the Merciless had moved to Mars and set up shop there. Naturally, after many challenges, Flash and his allies prevailed again.

Later, a 1951 science-fiction movie called *Flight to Mars* further deepened my interest in the red planet and the underground civilization that supposedly lived there. It helped that the plot and the graphics in that movie were a million times better than those in the Flash Gordon series.

I was able to combine my childhood fascination with science fiction with a serious desire to pursue scientific facts, thanks to a brilliant man who introduced me to the wonders of science and astronomy. Little did I know that my love for science would create a theological conflict with my friends at Bible Buzzards, where we were taught that many scientists were evil, arrogant people who had conspired to deceive the world with false theories about evolution and the age of the Earth that were contrary to God's revealed truth in the Bible. How was Flash Gordon going to get me out of this jam?

My Very Own Renaissance Man

Some people thought Edwin F. Bailey was weird. To me, he was strange in a million wonderful ways. His house was filled with books. Walking up the stairs of his house required navigating the various stacks here and there. His mind was filled with wonder for God's magnificent creation. I called him a modern-day Renaissance man because he had seemingly read something about everything, and no matter what topic was being discussed, he could bring additional information and insights. He was also musically inclined and played the sousaphone in the American Legion's marching band.

A devout Catholic, Mr. Bailey saw the world through the lens of faith. Even though he was largely self-taught, and thus technically an amateur in the world of science, his vast knowledge allowed him to lecture on astronomy at prestigious universities. Both he and his wife, the remarkable Eleanor Vadala Bailey, who was herself a distinguished scientist, welcomed me into their home. They mentored me and guided my growing mind. Together, they gave me much more than a trove of scientific information. They modeled a lifestyle that combined a deep devotion to God, a passionate curiosity about the workings of God's world, and a loving marriage that reflected a unique kind of intellectual equality between man and woman. They taught me to respect my mind and encouraged my hunger to apply my simple faith to the issues of the day.

For decades, Mr. Bailey worked for the Franklin Institute, a Philadelphia science museum and education and research center named after Benjamin Franklin. He founded the institute's Amateur Telescope Makers section, and when I was in the ninth grade, he taught me how to build my very own telescope, just like Galileo did. That telescope helped me place second in the Philadelphia Science Fair.

In those days, Philadelphia Science Fair winners were taken to the Institute for Advanced Study in Princeton, New Jersey, where the famous scientist Albert Einstein was on the faculty for more than twenty years. We were privileged to hear a lecture by Einstein on space-time relativity. The brilliant physicist promised to simplify his remarks for his youthful audience, but still, his lecture was way above my head.

Soon after that experience, Mr. Bailey offered me a part-time weekend job at the Franklin Institute as a tour guide and lecturer on meteorology and astronomy. He believed I was up to the job, and with his coaching, I soon was. But I later learned that part of the reason he had offered me the job was so he could spend more time with his beloved marching band.

Mr. and Mrs. Bailey helped me write out my lectures, which were based on lectures he had given, then worked with me to correct my poor grammar and bad pronunciation. Their investment in me would serve me well down the road, when I became a busy public speaker.

Every Saturday and Sunday afternoon for three years, I would go to the Franklin Institute, open the massive observatory roof, prepare the big telescope, help people see faraway parts of our cosmos, and answer their questions. I became an expert on sunspots and developed a talk on some of the fun things you can do with liquid oxygen. Even better, after I saw the movie *Flight to Mars*, I developed and delivered a lecture on space travel.

I was growing ever more fascinated by science, and the more I studied it, the more I could see how science reveals the details of God's work in creating everything in the cosmos, including you and me. As Mr. Bailey often explained, God and science were more than compatible. Genesis tells us what God did, and science tells us how God did it.

Crisis of Faith

My parents were proud of their Junior Galileo, and the people at our church mostly supported my interests. But my new career did not go over very well at Bible Buzzards, where I was told that scientists were God's enemies, that Charles Darwin was Satan's messenger, and that Mr. Bailey was sadly misinformed about religion and science being compatible.

The Bible Buzzards' leader had two major problems with science. For one thing, science said the cosmos was billions of years old, while the Bible said everything was created in the last ten thousand years. When I asked about where ancient fossils came from, or how the Colorado River carved the Grand Canyon in so little time, I received ready-made answers that failed to satisfy.

"God created those fossils and put them there," I was told. "And the Grand Canyon was carved by Noah. He hides such things from those arrogant enough to believe in foolish human wisdom."

The Bible Buzzards' second problem with science had to do with the creation of the human race. Science said humans had evolved over long periods of time, emerging from simpler forms of life. But the Bible Buzzards said that was heresy. God created the man and the woman in an instant, making the man from the dust of the earth, and creating the woman from the man's rib. To believe that humans evolved from monkeys or other forms of life over long periods of time would make humans into animals, contradicting the Bible's teaching that we are the crown of God's creation.

"Mr. Bailey is having a bad influence on you," they warned me.

At the time, I had never heard of cognitive dissonance, but I was experiencing a major case of it. I believed the Bible was God's truth, and I was committed to following its teaching. But I also knew that the Bible was not our only source of truth. Math was truth, too. Two plus two equals four, no matter what you believe about Jesus.

Speaking of two plus two, my youthful dream of growing up and becoming an astronomer soon died. Although they tried, it was not the Bible Buzzards who killed that dream. It was my pitiful aptitude for mathematics.

Reading God's Two Books

I would work out my cognitive dissonance by learning more about the history of Christianity. Over the centuries, different believers have embraced different approaches to dealing with science and faith. The Bible Buzzards said everything we need to know about life can be found through a literal interpretation of one book, the Bible. Science was unnecessary, and often false.

Mr. Bailey told me about Christian scientists and thinkers who, over the centuries, taught that God actually wants his people to read two books. The first book is the Bible, God's book of divine revelation. It tells us things that science and math could never determine, such as the nature of God, his love for creation, and how his love for us caused him to send his Son for our salvation. We read this book to find God's truth.

The second book is the book of nature, where we find truth through disciplines like science or math. Thousands of years ago, ancient people only knew how to read a few pages of this book. They understood when the seasons changed, and they could read the stars well enough to navigate on open water. In the past few centuries, science has enabled us to read many more pages of the book of nature. We now know more about the vast scope and the incredible intricacies of God's creation, both out there (the amazing cosmos) and in here (the microbiome within our own bodies).

The Bible Buzzards insisted the book of Scripture was in conflict with the book of nature. Mr. Bailey insisted they were compatible. The better I got to know both books, the more I became convinced that Mr. Bailey was right.

Theistic Evolution

My reading led me to a concept called theistic evolution, which emerged long before Charles Darwin published his *Origin of Species* in 1859. In 1692, an English cleric who was also a botanist, John Ray, published *The Wisdom of God Manifested in the Works of Creation*.

Theistic evolution is the view that God used and guided evolutionary processes to create the world's many creatures, including you and me. Theistic evolution is not random or purposeless, but is directed by God, the great Creator, to achieve his purposes. The more I studied God's two books, the more I saw how the evolutionary development described by science perfectly matches the sequence of creation spelled out in the early chapters of Genesis.

Instead of being forced to make an unnecessary choice between science and faith, I found a way to harmonize the two. What a relief! My cognitive dissonance about the natural world was resolved. Even better, I emerged from this conflict with my very own theological conviction that God wants his children to cherish and use the amazing minds he gave us. I'm so grateful that I did not let my love for the Bible Buzzards convince me to lock up my thinking in some cramped fundamentalist closet.

If I had gone in that direction, I might never have wound up studying and later teaching at Eastern Baptist College, which was then one of the few Christian colleges in America to have its own astronomy department and observatory. Science opened my mind to the hidden workings of God's creation. Once I had seen these glories, there was no going back.

I am grateful today as I write these words, but I am also grieving. I grieve because fundamentalists and evangelicals are still waging the same silly war against science that I encountered seventy years ago.

I grieve because millions of young people attending private Christian schools today are still being taught that science and faith are in conflict.

I grieve because, during a global pandemic, millions of Christ's followers opposed vaccinations and masks, even though such tools are part of God's provision for us, and even though such behavior needlessly endangered the lives of their neighbors, whom Christ commands us to love, as well their own lives.

Mark A. Noll was right in his 1995 book, *The Scandal of the Evangelical Mind*. He wrote: "The scandal of the evangelical mind is that there is not much of an evangelical mind." I saw the weakness of fundamentalist-evangelical teachings for myself during my crisis of faith over science. That experience led me to dedicate myself to carefully studying both of God's books for the rest of my life.

CHAPTER 7

CHURCH IN BLACK AND WHITE

New Berean Baptist Church held its congregational business meeting once a month right after the Wednesday evening prayer service. All members were welcome to attend, and many did. But for me, these meetings, at which church elders and deacons busily addressed various nonimportant issues, were tedious.

Boring was the rule, at least until March 1951, when one of our monthly meetings sparked controversy that drew media attention. I remember the time well because it came shortly after my family had thrown a great big party for my sixteenth birthday.

The cause of the uproar was race. A Black woman had attended New Berean for months. I did not know her, but I thought she was a beautiful woman whose dark skin stood out in our lily-white congregation. Now, after spending months meeting with our pastor, she had expressed her desire to join the church.

After a few preliminaries, our pastor, the Reverend Glenn Orr, stood up to start the monthly business meeting. "Is there any new business we need to address before we go to our agenda?" Pastor Orr asked. After hearing nothing from the gathering of about fifty people, he proceeded to the first item.

"Allow me to present my friend for membership at New Berean," he said, introducing the woman by name. He explained how he had met with her and discussed her faith in detail.

Typically, accepting new members into our congregation was a routine administrative matter that generated no controversy. Candidates for membership would testify to their faith in Christ and their desire to join our church family. Then the candidates would leave the room while we voted. Normally, pretty much everyone would vote to accept them, before inviting them back into the room, shaking their hands, hugging them, and welcoming them.

Not this time.

"I don't think we're ready for this kind of thing," said one of our church deacons, who stood and spoke with a tone of anger in his voice. "I oppose it."

I knew this deacon because his son was on the church basketball team. I remember him being upset when the Jewish boys joined our team. Most of them were better players than his son, who wound up spending more time on the bench than playing. This small-minded deacon always blamed the Jewish boys for his son's diminished status on the team.

Now he was going after a Black woman, and to my surprise, a number of church members agreed with him and echoed his ugly tone. Encouraged, the church deacon further explained why he wanted to reject the Black woman's request for membership.

"I know why she wants to join our church," he said, his voice growing louder. "She's a status seeker, and this is an attempt to improve her status. That's the motivation. It's not a desire to be a better disciple of Jesus Christ."

One man quickly made a motion to deny the woman membership.

"I second that motion," said another voice in the room.

Another person called for a vote.

"All in favor, say aye." Nearly all the voices joined in the chorus to oppose the woman's membership.

"All opposed?"

The room was silent except for one voice. Pastor Orr opposed the motion.

The vote was taken. The motion passed. The woman would not be allowed to join. New Berean would remain snow white.

The deacons wanted to move on to the next agenda item, but Pastor Orr had something to say first. "This is not about her status," he said. "This is about our status. It's about who we are as members of Christ's church."

Pastor Orr explained that the vote to exclude a believer from church membership because of her race was so contrary to his understanding of Scripture, and so contrary to what the Christian faith was all about, that he did not see how he could continue as the shepherd of our flock.

"Now that you have passed this motion, I have reached the unfortunate conclusion that the best thing for me to do now is to offer my resignation as your pastor," he said, before rising and quietly walking out of the room.

The next morning, the story that our church had denied membership to a Black woman made for an ugly newspaper story. Pastor Orr's departure was soon accomplished, and in time he found a position at another Baptist church not too far away.

None of us would ever see that Black woman in our church again, and most members were relieved that was the case. But for me, her rejection from our fellowship had been traumatic. As people would come to say during the 1960s, my consciousness had been raised.

Shock and Revulsion

To say I was shocked would be an understatement. I was in double shock, over both the rejection and Pastor Orr's resignation. I had always thought the people at New Berean were some of the most devout and loving Christians I knew. But now they had done something that struck me as profoundly un-Christian and even anti-Christian. I was too young and naive to have worked out any theology of race, but I felt deep down that they had done something wrong and unjust. Something seemed morally and spiritually wrong with my fellow congregants. The departure of Pastor Orr only added to my anger and despair.

During my years on the track team at West Philadelphia High School, I had come to know many of my Black teammates and to love some of them very much. Our shared love for our sport and our team broke down the barriers between us, and when we went out to compete against other schools, we were together as brothers, not divided by race.

In addition to my Jewish friends, I was around Black classmates all the time in high school. Some of them affectionately called me "Dove," for my white skin. And as student-body president, I felt obligated to serve all students, not just the students who looked like me.

I was not blind to the barriers that would pop up every time a Black person stood up to seek inclusion, respect, and equality. This was simply the way things were in the decades before America's civil rights movement took off. Signs of overt racism and race-based oppression were everywhere to see.

In the 1930s, when American boxer Joe Louis defeated German boxer Max Schmeling, Americans of all races cheered because our guy had beat up Hitler's guy. Louis would become a national hero, but he constantly faced racism outside the ring. When he beat popular Irish American Billy Conn, many whites concluded that the fight had been rigged.

When rumors flew that a popular entertainer was a racially mixed person passing as white, families around the country discussed mixed-race marriages and births around their dinner tables. Around our dinner table, the issue played out as you might expect. My mother thought the idea of mixed-race children was all wrong, while my dad did not see any problem in it.

Running through the center of West Philadelphia, Market Street functioned as a line of racial separation. Black people lived north of Market Street, while whites lived to the south.

Once Black families began to move into the neighborhoods to the south of Market Street, white flight began. Real-estate agents would go up and down the streets of white neighborhoods, warning homeowners to sell before more Blacks moved in and depressed home values. Many did so. As "For Sale" signs appeared up and down our street, it was sad to see old friends move away. A Black family eventually bought the house next door to ours, and they turned out to be wonderful neighbors.

Neither Jew nor Gentile

My friends at Bible Buzzards did not share my concern about the Black woman who was denied church membership. Some even accused me of embracing a "social gospel." That was the derisive term used by fundamentalists to describe what they considered to be an unholy prioritization of social concerns over theology.

Tom Roop and the other Buzzards felt that believers should focus on spiritual matters, such as evangelizing others and securing their salvation. This was the true gospel. They said only those who were lost, confused, or ignorant of the Bible would adopt a social gospel that focused on improving conditions in society.

Sure, it was wrong when Black men were lynched, or denied basic rights other Americans enjoyed, but it was not our job as Christians to change society. We were called to remain pure and unsoiled by the world's ways.

I asked Tom about Bible passages that talked about how all human beings are one in Christ. The New Testament says that on the Day of Pentecost, people of different races and nationalities spoke in tongues, showing that Christ's gospel was for all people.

The best-known passage is from Galatians, which Tom loved and regularly taught us: "So in Christ Jesus you are all children of God through faith, for all of you who were baptized into Christ have clothed yourselves with Christ. There is neither Jew nor Gentile, neither slave nor free, nor is there male and female, for you are all one in Christ Jesus. If you belong to Christ, then you are Abraham's seed, and heirs according to the promise" (Gal. 3:26–29).

When I read this passage, I saw Paul talking about how all of God's children—slave or free, male or female—were equal in Christ's sight and equally worthy of love and respect. But that's not the way Tom read it. He focused on the part about "neither Jew nor Gentile."

Tom talked to me about the Jewish temple and how Christ's death had torn the veil of the temple, breaking down the wall that had separated Gentiles from Jews and granting us access to God's love and mercy. For Tom, the passage was not about the equality of all people before God, but rather about the amazing things done by Christ to bring us closer to God.

Leaving New Berean

I understood what Tom was saying, but I still could not ignore my belief that my church had acted in an un-Christian manner by denying someone membership solely on the basis of her skin color. I came to the sad conclusion that New Berean was not the church for me. I needed to find another church.

One of the Black members of my high-school track team invited me to Mt. Carmel Baptist Church. I quickly fell in love with the rousing preaching and the warmth of the people. And I will never forget the powerful Good Friday sermon I heard delivered at Mt. Carmel by the church's longtime pastor, the Reverend Dennie W. Hoggard, with the memorable message "It's Friday, but Sunday's Comin'." I would later adopt this theme as my own, and I always did my best to channel Pastor Hoggard's inspiring delivery of that message.

Meanwhile, things did not turn out well for New Berean. The church remained closed to Black members, even as more and more Blacks moved into the surrounding neighborhood. Over time, membership declined, the last hymn was sung, and the church doors were closed. Ironically, the building was later reopened as the home of a Black church.

I never forgot the trauma of seeing a Christian woman cast out of our church because she was Black, and I would never again look at race and religion in the same way I had before. Before long, I would find myself studying at a Christian college where professors said Christ emphasized both loving God and loving your neighbor. This approach would help me develop a robust theology addressing the dazzling diversity of God's many children, which would guide my life for the next half century.

PART 2

ONE WHO CORRECTLY HANDLES THE WORD OF TRUTH

CHAPTER 8

LEARNING TO BE A CITIZEN OF GOD'S KINGDOM

I knew I wanted to go to college, but where? The question vexed me and kept me awake at night. On its radio show, King's College promised worried parents that it would send their young graduates back home with pretty much the same beliefs and ideas they had when they first arrived. That did not seem very educational to me. I wanted college to challenge and expand my thinking, not affirm everything I already knew.

Friends in Bible Buzzards suggested Moody Bible Institute, which prepared students for ministry. But I met some Moody grads at Bible conferences and felt they exuded a holier-than-thou attitude, as if saying, "We've got a handle on the truth, and nobody else does." I did not want to follow that approach, either. And I did not agree with Moody's dispensationalism.

Tom, the leader of Bible Buzzards, recommended Wheaton College in Illinois, but I doubted I was smart enough to succeed at the "evangelical Harvard." Plus, I needed to think carefully about costs since I would be paying for college myself with earnings from my many jobs.

A trusted friend and advisor told me about a new Christian school I had never heard of, located in a suburb of Philadelphia not far from my home. Eastern Baptist College was founded in 1952 by the same American Baptists who had established the affiliated Eastern Baptist Theological Seminary—known today as Palmer Theological Seminary—in the 1920s to train pastors.

My trusted advisor was Kent Holland, who had started dating my sister Rose when I was a senior in high school and would soon become her husband. Kent had just resigned from the United States Naval Academy in Annapolis in order to study at Eastern.

I loved Kent. He was a powerful role model for me: a tall, good-looking, athletic guy who had played on Navy's football team and was a deeply committed Christian. I would never have attended Eastern if he had not talked me into it. Kent was the sponsor of the Baptist Youth Fellowship at Eastern and coach of its undermanned basketball team. It felt good to be recruited. Even better, Eastern was inexpensive, and playing on the team decreased my tuition by six hundred dollars, which was a huge amount of money to me.

I thank God that Kent directed me to Eastern, which became such a big part of the rest of my life. The things I learned at Eastern would widen and deepen my faith in a million ways, preparing me for all kinds of ministry work that I never could have imagined or predicted. I started at Eastern in January 1953, a few weeks after I graduated early from high school, in the middle of the academic year. I joined Eastern's first class of undergraduates, and for the first time in my life, I began to think intentionally and seriously about what it meant to be a faithful disciple of Jesus.

Thinking Theologically

Before attending Eastern, I was like most Christian young people, cobbling together my faith out of bits and pieces of ideas I had picked up from those around me, including the differing theological views of my parents, hundreds of church sermons, the intensive Bible studies I was doing every week with the Bible Buzzards, and talks with my Jewish and Catholic friends.

All I knew was that I wanted to be like Billy Graham, and I felt the right Christian college would equip me for my calling. The Buzzards had persuaded me that the only way to please God was by spending the rest of my life working for him, either as a missionary to faraway places or as a pastor and evangelist, so I needed to prepare myself for that work.

I knew a couple of fancy-sounding theological words, like *eschatology* (the study of final things), but lacked any coherent understanding of where that fit into the bigger picture of faith. I had ideas and beliefs, but they seemed random and were stitched together only by my personal experience. I lacked any systematic understanding of Christian theology.

I was not prepared for the powerful ways my professors would help me enlarge my understanding of who Christ is and what he expects of us, leaving a powerful and lasting influence on my faith, intellectual development, and future ministry.

Kingdom Come, but How and When?

Robert W. Shinn was a brilliant man with a doctorate in church history who taught lively, penetrating classes on religion and philosophy at Eastern College. Dr. Shinn introduced me to a new concept: the kingdom of God. I had heard the words before, but now I learned what a central biblical theme this was. The Bible Buzzards taught that evangelism was a means of getting people into heaven when they died. Dr. Shinn helped me see that evangelism meant recruiting people to a movement through which God could begin to transform this world. God wants to establish his kingdom here on earth as it is in heaven, as we say in the Lord's Prayer.

We read John Bright's book *The Kingdom of God*, which was published in 1953 and is still in print and now draws rave reviews on Amazon. I began to see that throughout history God was at work in the world, creating a people who would in turn create a society in which God would be king and establish a social order that follows his will for us.

Put simply, God is at work in the world, transforming it from what it is into what he wants it to be. God's kingdom involves transformed people living in a transformed society, and this theology has plenty of implications for how Christians should live. This understanding became crucial to my thinking ever since my college days.

The dispensationalist theology I was taught through the Bible Buzzards claimed that history would end with the cataclysmic destruction of the earth, which is not a great inducement to work at making the world a better place. The Bible Buzzards believed that Christ would return soon and God's people would be delivered from this evil world, raptured to meet Jesus in the air.

The kingdom theology I was studying gave me a hope-filled eschatology that was quite different from the "end times" theology I had passively embraced before. God is at work *in our world*, and the kingdom of God will be realized in history and on earth, just as we hear every Easter in the "Hallelujah Chorus" of Handel's *Messiah*:

> The kingdom of this world
> Is become
> The kingdom of our Lord,
> And of his Christ;
> And he shall reign forever and ever.

We also read H. Richard Niebuhr's classic book, *Christ and Culture*, which described the five different ways Christians throughout history have engaged the dominant culture in which they lived. The concept that was most attractive to me was Niebuhr's "Christ as Transformer of Culture," a perspective that calls believers to engage the social order and do their utmost to transform it.

As Paul wrote to the church in Philippi: "I thank my God every time I remember you. In all my prayers for all of you, I always pray with joy because of your partnership in the gospel from the first day until now, being confident of this, that he who began a good work in you will carry it on to completion until the day of Christ Jesus" (Phil. 1:3–6).

Fundamentalists placed great emphasis on transforming individual people, but they largely ignored the transformation of societal structures. The opposite was the case for theological liberals. They emphasized transforming social structures but downplayed the importance of winning people into a personal relationship with Jesus Christ so that his Spirit could transform them into people fit to live in the kingdom of God.

Scholar of Note

Distinguished historian Dr. Lee Norcross Allen was a great teacher and a detail-oriented researcher, as I found out when I helped him compile footnotes for his doctoral dissertation in history at the University of Pennsylvania. Dr. Allen was teaching undergraduates at Eastern even as he was still finishing his PhD, a career path that I would soon copy. His dissertation dove deep into the life of William Gibbs McAdoo, a progressive presidential candidate in the 1920s.

Dr. Allen befriended me and mentored me, and the more I got to know about his research, the more I admired him. He became an intellectual role model for me. I was honored when he asked me to help him prepare an index for his dissertation. My job was to fill a stack of index cards with citation references, which was the system everyone used in those precomputer days. Hour after hour, he would call out each and every reference as it appeared in his paper while I wrote down the citation and the page number.

Helping Dr. Allen made me feel as if I had been welcomed into a sacred shrine to learning that was open only to a select few. I was permitted to look behind the curtain and see a master at work, witnessing the thoroughness with which he prepared his lectures and writings, which would serve me well when it came time for me to research my doctoral dissertation, lectures, and books.

But I was not a scholar yet, and I struggled in some classes. Greek would remain forever Greek to me, despite the encouragement of a professor who was overly generous in his grading.

Big Man on a Small Campus

I was not exactly the big man on campus, but thanks to my love of basketball, I was close enough. Eastern had a basketball team that was not too great, so I fit right in! I started as a guard on Eastern's team the week after classes began, and I remember our first game well. We were matched against Barrington College, and I scored ten points and had ten assists, becoming an overnight sensation on the little-heralded team. Eastern won more games than it lost that year, but that would be our last winning season during my years on the team.

My father attended my final basketball game in my senior year at Eastern. It was the only game of mine he ever saw. Happily, it was a nail-biter that resulted in a victory, and I was overjoyed that my dad saw me make the buzzer-beating, game-winning final shot, on a fast break following a steal. I still dream about that shot.

Fresh Wind

In one course on Christian classics, each student was asked to read one classic book. I chose John Wesley's journals because I wanted to understand his theology. What surprised me was how much Wesley wrote about the indwelling presence of the Holy Spirit in our lives.

Like me, Wesley worried about whether he was really saved. But under the influence of the Holy Spirit, he at last found the assurance of salvation he had sought, and his heart was "strangely warmed." His writing made it clear: you know you're saved if you feel the presence of the Spirit within you. This stood in contrast to the version of Calvinism I found in the notes of the Scofield Reference Bible.

Wouldn't you know it? Just as I was studying Wesley's descriptions of his spiritual experiences, I got to know some students at Eastern who were part of the emerging charismatic movement. I had heard plenty of traveling Pentecostal faith healers, but these charismatic folks were different. There was a warmth and vitality to these believers, who not only talked about the Spirit but also seemed to have fruits of the Spirit that had not yet ripened in me.

One Sunday I decided to join them. They asked me whether I wanted to be baptized in the Holy Spirit. I said yes, and they made a circle around me, laid hands on me, and prayed for the Holy Spirit to flow into me. I did not feel anything that night, but in subsequent nights as I prayed alone and waited in silence for God, I experienced something of the Spirit of Christ flowing into me.

Another time I attended a worship service led by the Reverend Randy Jones at a Pentecostal storefront church. Randy called people forward to pray to receive the Holy Spirit. That was the first time I have ever witnessed the phenomenon of praying in tongues. I loved the joy, energy, and singing of this Spirit-filled fellowship. I could not have experienced that at the Baptist church.

Still, the main thing I learned during this time in college was the spiritual value of silence. Before, my church life had been nonstop noisy. Now I was learning the spiritual discipline of listening. During my daily prayer times, I would devote time to silence and listening for God, and in some of those moments I began to feel the presence of God within me. Only much later would I develop a theology of prayer.

Silence remains an important part of my prayer times. I become very still and very quiet as I heed God's direction, as shared in the words of the psalmist: "Be still, and know that I am God" (Ps. 46:10).

Sometimes in prayer this soft, still voice speaks to me. And in some cases I can sense the guidance of the Spirit as I confront the challenges of life, which often seems like a never-ending series of important decisions.

Minding My Theology

As Mark A. Noll concluded, "There is not much of an evangelical mind." This remains as true today as it was when Noll made the statement thirty years ago. Today's evangelical movement is largely anti-intellectual, activistic, populist, pragmatic, utilitarian, and dominated by the urgencies of the moment, not the Christian traditions of the past.

This description is even more true of the fundamentalist movement in which I was raised. I grew up learning about a Jesus who asked a lot of questions, but I was not supposed to ask too many questions myself. Some Christian leaders saw questions as doubts or as insufficient respect for those in spiritual authority.

At Eastern, I had finally arrived in an environment where questions were honored and answers could be long-winded but revealing. Now, if only I could find an answer to the question that disturbed me more than all the others: What does God want me to do with my life?

CHAPTER 9

SEEKING MY CALLING

Pastor or missionary? Missionary or pastor? I was attending college to prepare for my future ministry, but I was having the hardest time figuring out what that ministry would be, and neither my friends, my professors, nor God seemed to be showing me the way. No matter what, I knew I was called to "full-time Christian service," as they called it in Bible Buzzards, and the two basic options were serving God here by pastoring a church or serving him "somewhere over there" in an unfamiliar place with no churches.

About half of all the young people involved in Bible Buzzards wound up choosing one of these two options, which is a tribute to Tom Roop, the hardworking layman who sacrificed his time to shepherd us kids. Tom constantly taught that salvation was a free gift, but once we received this gift, we were obligated to share it with others. Tom said we should be filled with a gratitude that motivates us to preach the gospel and to teach and disciple others. Our callings were not heavy burdens but joyful responses to the great gifts that God had given us in Jesus Christ. All of us earnestly sought to find our callings.

Years later, as I studied sociology, I would come to realize that there was another dynamic going on in the Buzzards. Tom was taking full advantage of his authority and of the power of the group to enhance the group members' conformity to his ideas. The obligation to full-time Christian service was taught so frequently and so powerfully that all of us got the message: If we do not do as Tom says, we will lose important social status in the group.

For me and other Buzzards, status in the group seemed equivalent to status with God. We all desperately wanted to check all the correct boxes that would earn us the reward we sought: God's approval. Tom was God's spokesman in our lives, so his approval was the next best thing. I wasted a lot of time, mental energy, emotional anxiety, and stomach acid trying to figure out what God was calling me to do, rather than trusting God to reveal it to me in his own good time.

Even though I had only been at Eastern for a brief time, I was already starting to change in profound ways. I was reading books by authors who had come from Christian traditions much different than my own, and I was meeting fellow students whose faith was different than mine.

I began to see that I had spent most of my life inhabiting a very narrow slice of the core of Christianity. At Eastern, I was gaining a better understanding of the breadth and depth of the body of Christ. And I was also becoming more critical of the narrow slice that had nurtured me for so long.

Get Thee a Mentor

I thank God for Herb Gilfow. Herb was the leader of Christian Endeavor, a powerful youth movement that was around long before Youth for Christ or Young Life. Herb had ministered to thousands of young people, gaining wisdom about how to deal with perplexed believers like me. He took an interest in me and gave me a brilliant piece of advice that changed the course of my life.

"Tony, if you really want to be a good minister of the gospel, you should find somebody who already is a good minister, attach yourself to him, and learn by observing everything he does."

I did not know then that I needed a mentor, but I did, and Herb recommended a pastor who would take me under his wing and gently guide me. I anxiously knocked on his office door one Saturday and was welcomed in. Thus began my pastoral on-the-job training, while I was still a young college student.

The Reverend John David Burton was the pastor of First Presbyterian Church in Mount Holly, New Jersey. He had impressive degrees from Princeton Theological Seminary and other esteemed institutions. Both First Presbyterian and Princeton were affiliated with the Presbyterian Church (USA), a denomination that my friends in the Bible Buzzards considered liberal or even heretical. But Dr. Burton embraced me and all of my fundamentalist and evangelical inclinations, seeing my arrival as a chance to inject some evangelistic energy into his well-established church.

I met him before I heard him preach. He had a weak speaking voice that sounded like a screech. Initially, I cringed at hearing him preach, but his content was so good that after a few minutes I completely forgot about how he sounded and became caught up in what he was saying. I loved his sermon illustrations, his brilliant organization, his expert use of the English language, and the sense of urgency he brought to every message. He was a craftsman of words and a published poet, as well as a pastor.

Only later would I come to see the hours and hours he spent in preparing each sermon, writing each one out by hand, word by word, then giving his copy to the church secretary, who typed it up and mimeographed copies so each church member could receive one on the way out the door.

After I had listened to him preach for about six months, he encouraged me to write my own sermon, which he evaluated and critiqued as I revised and reworked it. "This is going to be a good sermon," he told me. "Put it in the top drawer of your desk, and some Sunday I may call upon you to preach it."

Sure enough, my chance came a few months later when Pastor Burton came down with a case of laryngitis. I preached my sermon on the passage about Jesus and the rich young ruler in Mark's Gospel. Afterward, I shook hands with members at the back of the sanctuary as they left for home.

"That was a wonderful sermon," they told me. But Pastor Burton had warned me not to let the praise go to my head.

"The first one in line to praise you will be Satan," he warned.

Pastor Burton made himself available to me, and we often talked in the hallway before or after church for a minute or two. But it was our one-on-one meetings that had the greatest effect on me and showed me what a loving and caring man he was.

"I sense you are very serious about your Christian faith," he told me. "Where do you think this is going to take you? What form of Christian service is your calling?"

We talked for what seemed like hours and would continue to talk regularly as I worked alongside him for the next four years. He had a respect for evangelicals, but worried about independent fundamentalist churches, which he felt nurtured anti-intellectualism, legalism, judgmentalism, and meanness toward anyone who did not believe just as they did. I had to agree with him.

He was theologically orthodox. He thought an ideal education for a pastor would be an undergraduate degree from a good evangelical school like Wheaton, followed by further study at a mainline Protestant seminary like Princeton.

"It's important for a young man to have the zeal that fundamentalism generates," he said, "but it is also important to develop a theology of and commitment to the institutional church."

By his example, Dr. Burton taught me about the hard work required to be a pastor. He had an incredible work ethic, spending twelve-hour days in study and sermon preparation, managing the organizational affairs of the church, and visiting congregants. My workaholism mirrored his, and ever since working with him, I have marveled at casual and relaxed pastors who take a more hands-off approach to the job.

Pastoring 101 at First Presbyterian

Pastor Burton gave me regular assignments, which I embraced with gusto. I can remember going to visit shut-ins and feeling an urgency to make sure they knew about Jesus and had accepted him as their Savior.

I also threw myself into leading the junior-high and high-school youth groups, teaching lessons that harkened back to the detailed Bible studies we did at Bible Buzzards, though the energy was never as electric as it was with the Buzzards. Our high-school youth group had about twenty members when I started, but after three months of me calling every young person connected to the church, attendance grew to sixty-five. I tried to involve each of them in our lessons, singing, and fellowship. My emerging philosophy of youth work was to help young people feel secure in their leadership roles, and I let them run their own meetings on Saturday and Sunday evenings.

I believed that a dose of fundamentalism is a good thing for teenagers. As I knew from personal experience, fundamentalist sexual prohibitions can help protect young people with raging hormones from a heck of a lot of trouble.

Some ministers want to be the only stars in their congregations, but within three weeks of my arrival at First Presbyterian, Pastor Burton was introducing me to the congregation and giving me visibility in his Sunday services. These opportunities gave me a chance to be an evangelist, which is something I felt certain would be a major part of my calling.

"Mr. Campolo has been working with me, and I thought you should get to know him better," he told the congregation one Sunday. "I've asked him to read this morning's Scripture passage."

I loved the attention, but reading Scripture in public made me extremely nervous.

"Pastor Burton, I'm not very good at pronouncing things, particularly biblical names," I later told him with shame. "I'm coming out of an Italian family where my father spoke only a little broken English, and I'm nervous about sounding like that when I'm in front of your congregation."

He could see my weakness and fear and devised a brilliant solution. His wife, Jean, would tutor me, working with me on the biblical passages I would read for each Sunday morning's service.

When we felt I was ready, she and I would go over and unlock the church doors. I would ascend the church's majestic pulpit, and she would sit in the very last row of the church.

"You need to make sure I can hear and understand every word you say from way back here," she told me.

Our rehearsals happened on Saturday nights, which made for some late tutoring sessions, at least when Eastern's basketball team was in season. Sometimes after a big game I would not reach the Burtons' home until about 1 a.m., but Mrs. Burton was always waiting for me and ready to patiently prepare me for the next morning's readings.

So successful was her tutelage that in time I no longer needed it and could confidently read the Scripture passages on my own. But I will never forget the investment she made in me, an investment that would pay off later when I became a popular Christian speaker.

I would continue working alongside Pastor Burton throughout my college years at Eastern, and when it finally came time for me to graduate, he and Jean were there in the front row. When my name was called and I stepped forward to receive my diploma, they gave me a standing ovation. In truth, though, I should have given them a standing ovation, for loving me, guiding me, and helping me grow into the person God had created me to be.

Reaching the Unchurched

Churchgoing was mainstream during the 1950s, a decade when church membership grew at a faster rate than the population, rising from 57 percent in 1950 to 63 percent by 1960. Still, there were many Americans who did not attend church, and Pastor Burton wanted to reach them. That was my next assignment.

In the summer between my sophomore and junior years, I worked with the Monmouth Presbytery, walking door to door in nearby neighborhoods, asking people if they attended church, and inviting them to attend First Presbyterian. Pastor Burton would visit many of the families who were not attending any church.

This kind of face-to-face research was fascinating for me. I wanted to share the message of Christ with people, and the better I understood them and their possible reservations about Christianity, the better I would be able to say something that resonated with them.

After many anxious years spent trying to discern what God wanted me to do, I finally had an answer. I would serve God as a pastor of a local church. As soon as I had made that decision, a host of other decisions quickly fell into line. I began carefully choosing my courses at Eastern to prepare myself for my future work.

CHAPTER 10

PASTOR TONY

A year or two into my time serving alongside Pastor Burton at First Presbyterian Church in Mount Holly, my opportunities for ministry were expanding rapidly. That's because First Presbyterian was a big church that worked with and supported smaller churches in the area.

Before I knew it, I was working nonstop with other churches in the area, while continuing my studies at college and later at seminary. Doors were opening for me to serve, and I walked right through them and got to work.

In my door-to-door visits, somewhat to my surprise, many people said they would like to attend a new church. In response, I helped the presbytery launch a new congregation in Rancocas Woods, New Jersey.

Pastor Burton liked what I did there, so he asked me to take over a small church in Vincentown, in the pine barrens of New Jersey, called Retreat Chapel. I was helped there by Peggy Davidson, a fellow Eastern student I had begun to date and eventually married. (Given the combination of my modest means and heavy schedule, my early dates with Peggy usually entailed her coming along with me as I did my church work in New Jersey.)

Soon, Pastor Burton found a Princeton Seminary graduate to take over the pastoral duties at Retreat Chapel. That freed me for pastoral work at Jacksonville Presbyterian Church in Bordentown, New Jersey.

One day I was preaching at Jacksonville when I noticed two men in the congregation I had not seen before. After church, they approached me with a proposal. How would I like to continue preaching on Sunday mornings at Jacksonville, and then quickly drive over to their church, Chesterfield Baptist, to preach a second time there at a later Sunday service? I agreed and soon found myself commuting to New Jersey to preach in back-to-back services at different churches in different towns each Sunday morning.

One thing led to another, and my assignments overlapped. While working at Chesterfield Baptist, I helped to launch another Presbyterian church in Browns Mills, New Jersey.

Pretty soon I could see that the harder I worked, the more the work piled up. I began to understand a lesson Jesus taught his disciples. Large numbers of people followed Jesus wherever he went, and as he looked at these people Jesus could see their pain, as Matthew's Gospel shows.

"When he saw the crowds, he had compassion on them, because they were harassed and helpless, like sheep without a shepherd. Then he said to his disciples, 'The harvest is plentiful but the workers are few. Ask the Lord of the harvest, therefore, to send out workers into his harvest field'" (Matt. 9:36–38).

I could see a plentiful harvest all around me—people who had no real commitment to God and no connection to a church other than attending an Easter or Christmas service. I was doing everything I could to reach these people, but I often felt as if I was carrying too much of this burden on my own.

Ecclesiology 101

Although these busy years offered little time for deep theological reflection, the combination of my studies at Eastern and my church ministry informed my theology on many issues, especially my ecclesiology, or theology of the church. I began to develop a solid ecclesiology by studying what the Bible, theologians, and church history and tradition tell us about Christ's church. This was something I had never studied much before. Dispensationalists gave little priority to the church, seeing it only as a parenthetical way station between the church of Laodicea and the establishment of God's kingdom.

I had grown up hearing about church as fellowship, but I came to see church as more than simply a fellowship of one group of people in one place. I could now see the church as the universal, mystical body of all those people who love and follow Christ. I began to understand the Holy Spirit's movement within the fellowship of believers. I also developed a better understanding of the role that sacraments and other church rituals play in nurturing the spiritual well-being of the church's membership. I had always taken Sunday Communion, but now I developed a richer appreciation for this sacrament.

My busy schedule also gave me a wealth of preaching experience. Following the model of my mentor, Pastor Burton, I would devote many hours to preparing sermons, focusing on making them interesting and worthwhile. My preaching benefited from my hands-on ministry, and the sorrows and fears that people confessed to me inspired many a sermon. I also benefited from the conversations I had with people about faith when I knocked on their doors.

I recognized that every sermon needs a structure. I usually relied on the common form of three carefully defined points that would carry the theme. I tried to provide a good story to illustrate each of the points, as well as a good conclusion in which I would call upon the people to act, to do something as a result of hearing the sermon.

My goal for my sermons was simple. The effectiveness of each sermon would not be measured by how many members complimented me or said "Amen" to some of my points, but by the extent to which people became "doers of the word and not hearers only."

As James spelled out in his epistle: "Do not merely listen to the word, and so deceive yourselves. Do what it says. Anyone who listens to the word but does not do what it says is like someone who looks at his face in a mirror and, after looking at himself, goes away and immediately forgets what he looks like" (James 1:22–24).

Emphasizing Evangelism

Baptists said they were committed to evangelism, but that did not mean they were always successful in reaching unbelievers. Mainline Presbyterians did not emphasize evangelism at all. In all the time I worked with him, I never heard Pastor Burton give an invitation for people to accept Christ. But everything I did was evangelistic at that stage of my life. I wanted to make sure everyone in the pews and everyone I visited at home or in the hospital was saved. Most of my sermons at First Presbyterian included invitations for people to receive Christ as their Savior. Pastor Burton never objected.

You can imagine my excitement when I learned that Billy Graham, my evangelical hero, would lead a crusade at Madison Square Garden in 1957. Graham understood that the fields were white (meaning ready) to harvest (John 4:35). He was doing all he could to evangelize the entire nation when few churchgoers seemed equipped or motivated to bring anyone, even their own neighbors, to Christ.

So far I had only seen Graham preach on TV, but I knew he was also working behind the scenes to reform fundamentalism and replace it with something called evangelicalism. In 1956 he had helped to found a magazine, *Christianity Today*, to promote this reform.

Fundamentalists believed there was only one true church, but Graham believed that God was at work in many churches. He invited Catholics, Episcopalians, and mainstream Protestants to participate in planning his crusades.

I asked the members of Chesterfield Baptist Church if they wanted to attend the crusade, and about fifty members said yes. We rented a bus and traveled to New York, sitting in the balcony where we had a good view of the place, which was packed. Some skeptics had predicted that the country boy would flop in the big city, but so many people continued to turn out for Graham's rallies that he extended his New York crusade from six to sixteen weeks, the longest in his career.

Seeing Graham in person was electrifying. He was a dramatic and dynamic preacher whose very presence commanded my attention. He was tall and handsome and had wonderful, flowing blond hair that I admired. I was already going bald and would wake up every morning with hair all over my pillow.

At the conclusion of his rousing and convicting sermon, Graham issued his invitation, asking anyone who wanted to receive Christ as Savior to walk to the front of the stage as Graham's music director, Cliff Barrows, led the choir in singing "Just as I Am." Immediately thousands of people streamed toward the platform, including a few from our church group. It was exciting to see so many respond to Graham's message, but I was also conflicted.

I had already walked down aisles many times to receive and reaffirm my salvation, so I knew the feeling. But was there a commitment that went beyond feeling? It seemed easy for people to say yes to Jesus, but it was much more difficult for them to grow spiritually and show the fruits of Christian living.

Jesus has many followers, but he desires disciples who will follow him and do what he says. As John Wesley famously said, "The church changes the world not by making converts but by making disciples."

From Baptisms to Funerals to Fights

My church work let me discover that I loved youth ministry, and during my time at Mount Holly and other churches, the youth groups I led grew. Youth work did not seem like work to me. It felt natural to relate to young people about Jesus, leading me to wonder, "Wouldn't it be great if I could do this for the rest of my life?"

I also remember very sad times when I sat at the bedsides of people who were dying. I knew how to quote Scripture about life and death, but my explanatory bromides seemed empty at moments when people confronted eternity. This was very hard, but the worst part was seeing how death affected the lives of those left behind. As a pastor, I became acquainted with grief.

Much of the grief I witnessed was inflicted by Christians on their fellow Christians by spreading dissension in the church. I learned that the fact that such pain was avoidable did not make it any easier to bear when it came.

I walked into a difficult situation when I responded to an invitation to apply for a pastor's position at Bridgeport Baptist Church near King of Prussia, Pennsylvania. This church would be a culture shock for me. A significant number of church members said they no longer wanted to be affiliated with the American Baptist Church, which they felt was too liberal. American Baptists were members of the National Council of Churches and the World Council of Churches, and some church members opposed those affiliations. They wanted to be part of an independent Baptist church instead.

Because I was still relatively green as a pastor, I underestimated the power of church conflict and fooled myself into believing that I could bring about a truce between the two sides. I would gradually learn the error of my ways, but not before I almost had a nervous breakdown from the accumulating tension, ill will, and anger.

How could brothers and sisters in Christ treat one another this way? This would be one of the many topics I discussed at length with my increasingly close confidante, Peggy Davidson.

CHAPTER 11

OUR FAMILY VALUES

We called it "The Bachelors' Club." We were a serious group of four guys at Eastern Baptist College who pledged to go overseas and serve as missionaries together. As we saw it, our singleness was a sign of our faithfulness to Christ and our commitment to his holy mission for our lives. As bachelors, we thought that we could never be tempted away from God's higher call by getting married, something that neither Jesus nor Saint Paul did. Our favorite verse was one of Paul's: "It is good for them to stay unmarried, as I do" (1 Cor. 7:8).

We bachelors gathered for lunch as often as we could, led by a student named Merritt Whitman, who was my teammate and the star of Eastern's basketball team. Often, our bachelor professor Lee Allen would join us for lunch.

Our commitment to remaining single not only prepared us for our service but also signaled to others our superior spirituality. We would never give in to the lusts of the flesh that lure weaker men into marriage. While I saw marriage as a hindrance to ministry, I was Italian, and it was important to get married and have a male offspring to carry on the family name. And my commitment to solitary life would weaken significantly as I grew closer to Peggy.

When Opposites Attract

Peggy and I met at Eastern in 1956, the year before Buddy Holly had a big hit with his song "Peggy Sue":

> If you knew Peggy Sue
> Then you'd know why I feel blue
> Without Peggy, my Peggy Sue

I really liked Peggy, even if my extremely extroverted personality was a major contrast to that of this quiet, pretty freshman. Above all else, I was attracted to Peggy because she was a very kind person.

"I came from a Scottish-Irish family," Peggy remembers. "I had wonderful parents who provided everything I needed—except for excitement. Then along comes this wild Italian man who was making waves everywhere. I had only been at Eastern a short time before I became aware of this guy who had a party happening around him every time he came into a room."

The two of us had many differences, but I liked that Peggy was a pastor's daughter. Her father, uncle, brother, and a cousin were all esteemed Baptist ministers. I felt that her family experience would help her understand me and the demands of a career spent in ministry. But it was not long before I discovered that Peggy had no interest in marrying a man of the cloth. "Hundreds of girls went to Eastern to marry a pastor, but I wasn't one of them," she says. "As a pastor's daughter, I saw my dad working every weekend and being required to be out at night too. That was the last thing I wanted."

Peggy was less sure about her salvation than I was about mine. She had been raised in a home and church culture in which people who had doubts about their faith were encouraged to pretend that all was fine. That's what she did, but the promised assurance of salvation did not seem to follow. Unlike me, who tried to deal with my doubts by walking down church aisles to accept Christ's salvation time and time again, Peggy kept her doubts to herself, hoping they would pass. It was a very long time before they did.

None of these differences prevented our love from growing stronger, and we spent more and more time together as the months passed. Soon love overcame our differences, and by Christmas of my senior year we were engaged. We broke up early the next year, but got engaged again by Christmas 1957 and finally married in 1958. For us, marriage was a forever thing, not a test run we could end if things did not work out. We knew we would be together forever, and now, more than sixty-five years later, we're still approaching forever together.

Competing Visions

People grow up absorbing all kinds of different concepts and romantic notions about what marriage should be. I had my ideas about what a pastor's wife should be like: selfless, sacrificial, accomplished on piano and organ, outgoing and welcoming with church members and visitors, and fully supportive of me.

After many years of hearing sermons and engaging in Bible studies, I knew all about the characteristics of the ideal woman and wife. First and foremost, she should be a "help meet" for me, just like God said back in the Garden of Eden. "And the LORD God said, It is not good that the man should be alone; I will make him an help meet for him" (Gen. 2:18, KJV).

I believed that the more submissive a wife was, the better. Peggy quickly disabused me of this notion, even though she did her best to help me. She played the piano, not the organ, but she agreed to play an old pump organ I found for us to use in a new church we were starting in a fire station. On Sunday mornings the firemen would move the trucks out, and we would move in the chairs and the old organ. Peggy gave that contraption all she had, pumping the pedals with both feet as her fingers played the keys. The only problem was that one of the keys—a D one octave above middle C—got stuck every time she played that note, meaning that each hymn was interrupted by an annoying D note until Peggy could grab the key and pull it back up into its normal position.

If asked, I would have said I subscribed to a "traditional" approach to marriage, with the man as the undisputed head of the house. But the meaning of "traditional" changes over time, and the fact is I never had a class at Eastern on family. I never studied the topic of family until I took a class on the sociology of the family when I started my PhD. In many ways, early on in my marriage with Peggy, I did not know what I believed about the role and structure of a Christian family.

In the course I took on the sociology of the family, I learned that I had grown up in a "matrifocal" family, meaning that the wife is the actual head of the home. If my dad put his foot down on any given issue, my mom would have given in to him. But he was not one to make everyday decisions, so Mom did that.

Peggy and I developed a relationship that became more egalitarian. We agreed early on that neither of us would make decisions unilaterally. As things worked out, Peggy would come to make many decisions for both of us.

We shared roles that other people defined as either "men's work" or "women's work." Peggy managed the family's finances—something for which I had no skill or patience. And there were times when I would be inside scrubbing the floors while she was outside mowing the grass.

Peggy had her own ideas about the ideal husband. She expected me to be more like her father, who was not only a good pastor but a loving family man who took good care of their house and all of their possessions and knew how to fix things when they broke. I had not developed this particular handyman skill set, and I never did.

Peggy's picture of the ideal marriage was a calm domestic life. She hoped that I would go off to do my work during the day and then come home to spend quiet evenings with her. But all I knew was a nonstop life that had me working or studying nearly every hour of the day. How could I do anything less than be a workaholic when the eternal destiny of souls at risk was at stake?

Our marriage was rich in love but low on cash, which worried me to no end, since I grew up in a home in which the head of the house did not make enough money to support our family of five. My measly pastor's salary did not even provide well for our penny-pinching family of two. I had the mindset that a preacher should have no materialistic desires. To ask for money was not something preachers did. We preached for the sheer privilege and duty of delivering God's Word. In the future, my perspective on this point would affect our family very severely.

Money was incredibly tight—so much so that I griped at Peggy for buying a simple manual can opener. Instead of complimenting her for saving money by skipping the more expensive electric can opener, I asked her, "Why buy a can opener when we can get a beer-can opener for free, and that works just as good?"

Stretching every cent was stressful but necessary. We served small country churches attended by farmers who rarely had any money for the collection plate, but helped keep us alive with their gifts of eggs, tomatoes, and sweet corn. It was a stressful time as we watched the money we had received at our wedding slowly disappear to cover our living expenses.

On the plus side, we enjoyed living in a cute little farmer's tenant house next to a big pasture that would have made a great Thomas Kinkade painting. In time, we city slickers would learn a few farm tricks. Peggy once showed up at a nearby barn at 5 a.m. to learn how to milk a cow. I survived a few stifling hours working inside a dust-filled, 100-degree silo as farmers dropped off their grain for storage.

Peggy worked tirelessly to fulfill all the expectations people place on a pastor's wife. "I tried to do everything my mother had done," she said. Even though she was an introvert, she worked overtime to make friends with everyone in the church. And when church members did what church members often do—calling their pastor at all hours looking for help with an urgent crisis—Peggy fielded the calls and counseled people as best she could whenever I was out.

The two of us enjoyed being deeply involved in a tight-knit community we were helping to sustain and grow. We started a successful Vacation Bible School program, and Peggy taught first grade at a local country schoolhouse. We even launched a pretty good Little League baseball team. Our pitcher, who looked much older than his age, pitched a furious fastball that hardly anyone could hit. As his renown grew, some opposing coaches started asking to see his ID so they could make sure he was not an undercover college player.

Love, Marriage, and Baby Carriages

Peggy and I disagreed about many things, including when to have children, and we worked to arrive at a solution we could both accept. I wanted to wait until I finished seminary and had a pastoral position that paid enough to support a growing family. Peggy had a different timeline.

"All the women my age had cute houses and cute babies," Peggy recalls. We had the house part, but not the baby part of the picture. Peggy wanted that to change.

Lisa came along two years after we married. Bart followed three years later. Before they were born, I envisioned children as inevitable interrupters of my studies, but as soon as I held Lisa in my arms, I melted. I quickly saw how miraculous childbirth is and came to appreciate my two wonderful kids.

Lisa loved flying kites. When she was little, she and I would go to a field in front of the Upper Merion Church, where I was then a pastor, to fly a kite. I would get the kite up in the air and then give her the string. Typically, she would hold the string and fly the kite for a few minutes before deliberately letting go, which forced me to chase after the string and save the kite. She enjoyed seeing me frantically run around more than she enjoyed flying the kite.

When Bart was a young boy, his passion was professional car races. During race season, Bart and I would leave church after services on Sunday morning and head right for one of the region's many racetracks—in Trenton, New Jersey; Langhorne, Pennsylvania; Dover, Delaware; or Pocono Raceway in the Pennsylvania mountains. One time we even saw Mario Andretti, the famous Italian-American driver. In coming years I would speak to many different audiences, but from Bart's boyhood perspective, I never made it to the big time because I never prayed the opening invocation of the Indianapolis 500 race.

The adventures with the kids came later, though. First, I had to adjust to the realization that we were now a family of four. This dramatically increased the pressure I felt to "man up" and provide for my family. I know I was not alone in feeling the pressures of new family responsibilities. Parenthood was a big adjustment for Peggy and me, as it is for any young couple. But we have loved our children dearly, and both have stretched us and changed us in amazing ways.

Not the Only Lisa and Bart

Over the years, Lisa and Bart provided me with plenty of humorous stories I would later use in my speaking career, but sometimes when I started talking about my two children I would hear some listeners snicker and laugh. The snickering was inspired by a now-famous animated family that stars in one of TV's longest-running scripted primetime shows.

TV's Bart and Lisa Simpson are nothing like our Bart and Lisa. Our Bart was never the devious brat we see on TV. Our Lisa has never played the saxophone. But there's one similarity pretty much everyone can agree on. I look a lot like Homer.

CHAPTER 12

FAITH IN BLACK AND WHITE 2.0

The headline spread across the front page of the hometown newspaper in Norristown, Pennsylvania, carried an ugly story about local men who had been arrested in an Alabama civil rights demonstration. The photo showed two Northeasterners in a sea of Black faces. Both were members of Upper Merion Baptist Church in King of Prussia, Pennsylvania, the church I led.

One of the men was a prominent deacon in our church. The other was Paul Stagg, an executive with our American Baptist denomination, which had just relocated its headquarters to an office about half a mile from our church. Paul was among the denominational leaders who joined our congregation; as is often the case, denominational leaders can be a bit more progressive than the people in the pews.

Paul tried to live his life according to his faith. After the Supreme Court ruled in *Brown v. Board of Education* that segregated public schools were unconstitutional, many white Christians in the South fled public schools for segregated Christian academies. But Paul's two daughters attended public schools in Virginia alongside Black kids.

Now it was the early 1960s, and Paul and other denominational workers were joining Upper Merion Baptist Church. Many supported the civil rights movement, which was spreading across America. It had been just a few years since Rosa Parks had refused to sit in the back of the bus and the young pastor Martin Luther King Jr. had organized the Montgomery bus boycott.

Many whites remained uncertain, fearful, or defiantly opposed to civil rights for Blacks, but Paul Stagg traveled south to work with Dr. King. Like all who volunteered to help the effort, Paul went through the required training in nonviolent resistance. This taught protesters to remain calm even when they were attacked or spit on by opponents, bit by police dogs, or arrested by police and thrown into jail. They would not respond with violence or anger. Paul would march alongside Dr. King and be arrested with him.

I was proud to see two members of my flock committing themselves to the cause of racial equality and doing something about it, even if that meant risking their lives and reputations. But not all members of our church shared my appreciation for their activism. In time, disagreements about race and other issues would divide our congregation and bring my work as a pastor to a premature end.

Our Church's Most Vocal Racist

One of our church's longest-serving deacons would never be caught dead doing anything to help Black people, whom he referred to with racist slurs. He was vociferously opposed to any of them buying houses in his segregated neighborhood.

It was not lost on this particular deacon that his pastor was on the opposite side of this issue. The more I learned about racial injustice, the more passionate I became. I was not trying to be political, but simply trying to be faithful and apply clear biblical teaching on the equality of all of God's children.

Early on, community members invited me to join them in their protests of racial discrimination at Philadelphia's Girard College, which was founded in 1848 as a private high school to serve poor, white, male orphans. By the 1950s, Girard's surrounding neighborhood was majority Black, but the school refused to admit any Black students. After years of protests outside its tall stone walls—and a Supreme Court decision—Girard College finally admitted its first four Black students in 1968. Today, Black students are the majority at Girard (and the exclusions of women and non-orphans have also been long-since dropped).

Later on, I teamed up with a local Presbyterian minister and other clergy to organize the Fair Housing Council of Upper Merion Township. Our goal was to help Black people find fair housing. There was a nearby General Electric facility that had hired many Black engineers, who were making good money but could not buy homes for their families. Among the obstacles they faced were people like my racist deacon, as well as banks and real-estate agents who refused to deal with them.

Our local Fair Housing Council adopted the tactics of similar councils around the country and used undercover operations to expose real-estate agents and mortgage lenders who were breaking the law by discriminating against Black buyers. We worked with a Black couple, arranging for them to go to a real-estate agent's office and inquire about available housing. Within about ten minutes they were told no housing was available. Then we followed up with a white couple, and they were told that many nice properties were on the market.

We tape-recorded both meetings and then got to work. First, we wrote a complaint and took it to the state capital. Next, we notified the Norristown *Times Herald*, which printed a front-page story. We were gaining the attention we wanted, but there was a price. Our efforts generated tension in our tight-knit community. The local Rotary Club canceled its invitation to host me as a speaker—something I would experience again, decades later, when another controversy arose over my stance on the church's treatment of gay people.

A Generational Confrontation

Our Fair Housing Council was so successful in fighting the real-estate market's entrenched racism that Black families soon started buying houses locally. In fact, we succeeded beyond our expectations. One Black family bought the house right next door to the loudly racist deacon in my church.

It was my habit to greet new families in the neighborhood. When I met the new Black family, I found them wonderful, but their church deacon neighbor believed they were lower than animals. He soon got so fed up with me that he quit attending church altogether. I went to visit him at his home one afternoon to encourage him to start attending church again. He had no interest in that and pressed me about why I was "stirring up trouble with the coloreds."

I reminded him that the Bible says God created all people, and that all tribes and clans and races were equally his children and will gather together to praise God in heaven, as the book of Revelation says.

He argued that God created different kinds of humans with a plan to elevate some to positions of authority and leadership over others who were destined to lives of perpetual servitude to their superiors. At the time, many white Christians held racist beliefs, but few would broadcast their hatred as loudly and passionately as this particular deacon did.

I let him know that I believed his views were an affront to our Creator God and to Christ's gospel. "I came here to try to get you back into the church," I said, "but listening to you talk, I don't think that's a good idea. We're trying to build a church that loves and welcomes anybody God brings our way. If you don't believe that, maybe you *shouldn't* come back."

My comments only increased his rage, and soon he was escorting me to the front door. As I was walking through the front room, I looked up to see his teenage son, Jerry, who had listened to our argument from the top of the stairs. Like his dad, Jerry had been absent from church for some time, but he surprised me by showing up alone the next Sunday.

At the end of my sermon that morning, I did what I always do: I gave an invitation for people to come forward and accept Christ as their Savior. Jerry stood up, walked down the aisle, knelt at the altar, and gave his life to Christ.

When I talked to Jerry the next week, I learned that he had long opposed his father's racial hatred. He explained that part of why he had stopped attending church was that he did not like to see the church provide a safe haven for people, like his father, who clung to the kinds of race-based prejudice that Jesus opposed in his teaching and ministry. This would not be the last time that I saw young people grasping and applying Christian principles to sing songs that their tradition-minded parents did not have ears to hear.

From then on, Jerry's life took a different direction. His faith continued to grow. He wound up meeting and marrying a wonderful Lutheran girl. In time he was called to the pastorate. The last I heard, he was leading a Lutheran church in Arizona.

Crying in the Dark

These were tough times for me. I believed God had called me to be a pastor, and I was pursuing that calling with all of my heart. But my heart was repeatedly broken by the many problems I confronted all around and within me.

As a pastor, I discovered two important facts about myself. First, I absolutely hated church administration and details. I loved participating in worship services and other church gatherings, but was ground down by the logistics required to make these gatherings a success. Neither our fundraising nor bookkeeping were as robust as they should have been. And of course, I hated being the one who was blamed whenever anything went wrong at church.

Second, I hated divisions within the church and grieved over my inability to bring people together around the core beliefs and practices we share as Christians. No matter how much I prayed and worked, I failed to navigate the politics of the church.

One political battle had started long before I became Upper Merion Baptist's pastor. The church decided to shift its mission focus in order to support independent missionaries, rather than missionaries affiliated with the American Baptist denomination, which was a member of the National Council of Churches, an organization committed to positive social change. The fundamentalists in my congregation did not appreciate the warm welcome I was giving to denominational employees like Paul Stagg.

Another battle surrounded my pastoral visitation work. I offended a faction of the church by spending too much time visiting new people who were moving to our town and making the church grow by leaps and bounds. They said I should focus my visitation on existing members of the church, who felt neglected as I sought new members.

I was even blamed when two couples who had been members for years both left within six months. What I could not tell those who complained was that, in both cases, the couples faced painful personal problems involving other members of the church community, and after extensive counseling with me, the couples decided to leave the church, start afresh elsewhere, and receive more counseling.

In some ways, my studies at Eastern Baptist Theological Seminary had only made matters worse for me. The more I studied church history and theology, the more I came to understand the beauty and glory of the church, Christ's body on earth. The more I learned about what the church could be and should be, the more frustrated I grew by the reality I faced, navigating tensions and dissension in the churches I served. The dichotomy between my theology of the church and the realities of daily church life was growing larger by the day.

One day I was looking in the parsonage attic when I came across a collection of ten angry letters addressed to the previous pastor. While it was comforting to know that many of the problems I was facing at Upper Merion Baptist had been faced by previous pastors, I also realized that much of the trouble in the church was my own doing, and that made me incredibly sad. My inability to find harmony between opposing factions forced me to see that, as an inexperienced pastor in my twenties, I lacked the wisdom, spiritual maturity, life experience, and emotional intelligence I needed to shepherd my flock well.

Some Saturday nights, I would go out late and sit alone behind the church building in the dark, silently crying to myself as I asked God, "What do you want to do with me? How can I serve you?"

God would quickly answer my prayer, but I did not appreciate the way he did so.

Déjà Vu

The final straw came when a Black college student from Eastern who had been attending our church sought to join and be admitted as a full-fledged member. We decided to address the student's request at our next Wednesday night business meeting.

One deacon had warned me that the meeting might not go well and that I should try to keep my cool. I held out hope that the believers I had been leading and teaching for more than a year would do the right thing. That hope died as soon as our vociferously racist deacon showed up and loudly proclaimed his ugly views, starting with his customary racial slur and asserting: "These people should stay with their own kind."

I was angered that he would say such things in God's house, and I rose to respond, quoting the moving lines from the apostle Paul's letter to the believers in Galatia: "So in Christ Jesus you are all children of God through faith, for all of you who were baptized into Christ have clothed yourselves with Christ. There is neither Jew nor Gentile, neither slave nor free, nor is there male and female, for you are all one in Christ Jesus. If you belong to Christ, then you are Abraham's seed, and heirs according to the promise" (Gal. 3:26–29).

"If we close the doors of our church to this student, we are turning our back on the church's mission," I said in a final effort to influence the vote.

But all was in vain. A significant majority of the members of the church I led denied membership to the Black student.

It was déjà vu for me. A decade earlier, our family's New Berean Baptist Church had taken a similar vote and excluded a Black Christian from joining the church. I was sixteen years old back then and did not really have any theological understanding of race. Since then, I had gained a much deeper understanding of the Bible's teaching on the fundamental equality and inherent dignity of every person created in the image of God.

Now that my flock had voted to deny membership to a Black person, I knew I needed to follow the example of Pastor Orr, the principled pastor who resigned from New Berean over its racist vote.

"It has been my honor to serve as your pastor at Upper Merion Baptist Church," I told them, "but if this is your choice, I must resign as your pastor."

I grabbed Peggy's hand, and we rushed out of the meeting.

From "Pastor Tony" to "Professor Tony"

I still wanted to be a pastor, but I did not see how I could do it anymore. This left me in a personal, professional, and spiritual dilemma. I loved Jesus and was studying theology at seminary, but I no longer felt God calling me to be a pastor. Little did I know that my pastor's pulpit would soon be replaced by a professor's podium.

The vote at Upper Merion Baptist Church was taken on a Wednesday evening. The next Friday morning, I gathered copies of my résumé and went to visit three local colleges to see if they might need a new faculty member. I visited the schools that are today known as Cheyney University of Pennsylvania, a historically Black university, Delaware County Community College, and Eastern University.

Eastern was the only school to express interest in me and brought me on board in 1964. I would spend the next half century serving my alma mater.

PART 3

HUNGER AND THIRST FOR RIGHTEOUSNESS

CHAPTER 13

DOUBLE VISION

Attending college at Eastern was just what I needed. I grew in my faith, learned so much about Christian teaching and theology, enjoyed being part of a vibrant college community, and met Peggy. But even after graduating, I knew I still had major theological deficits. My years of leading churches had revealed just how poorly I understood many important issues. I was humbled, seeking new ways to serve God, and hungry to know more about his truth. It was time to go deeper in my theological education.

Even though I was raised as an American Baptist, I had my heart set on attending the large Southern Baptist Theological Seminary in Louisville, Kentucky, because of its academic reputation and its strong faculty. Plus, I would be able to attend tuition-free.

I had worked hard at my various jobs and saved up what money I could to buy a car I called Gargantua. It was a used 1946 Buick that was as big as a battleship and had a cool torpedo back. I loved big cars, and even by American standards, Gargantua was gigantic.

On the night before I was scheduled to leave for Kentucky, I packed that car full of everything I thought I might need for my first year at seminary and went to bed. But early on Monday morning, my mother woke me up, desperate for help. "I don't know what to do!" she said. "Your father has been writhing in agony all night!"

My father, whose health had been declining for years, had suddenly taken a turn for the worse. At night the whole household was awakened by the sound of his groans. He had Hodgkin's disease, now known as Hodgkin's lymphoma, a type of cancer that attacks the lymphatic system, which is part of the immune system.

A doctor came to see Dad on Monday, and the news was bad. "It's only going to go downhill from here," the doctor told us. There was no available cure, and Dad would need ever-increasing doses of morphine to dull the pain that wracked his body.

In an instant, my seminary plans changed. With my father struggling and approaching the end of his life, this was not a time to move almost seven hundred miles away. I would instead attend nearby Eastern Baptist Theological Seminary. Dad would spend his last days at Lankenau Hospital in Wynnewood, Pennsylvania, which was a little more than two miles down the road.

I was sorely disappointed as I unpacked Gargantua, and I was sorrowful for my dad. But God works in mysterious ways, and in time I would see that the decision to attend seminary at Eastern was a major fork in the road for me, a decision that would affect the course of everything I would do later in my life, including public speaking and writing books.

Eastern gave me a unique chance to study theology. And thanks to a scholarship offered to Eastern students, I could also study at two other fine institutions, the University of Pennsylvania and Temple University.

I chose to study sociology as well as theology, believing that studying both God's Word and God's world would give me training in two disciplines and provide me with the "double vision" I could use for the rest of my life to explore the problems facing our society and the responses Christians can make to these challenges.

A Feast for a Hungry Mind

Mornings and afternoons, I studied theology at Eastern, diving deep into church history, biblical interpretation, and the kingdom of God—a subject that had obsessed me as an undergraduate. I saw that Christ taught his followers to promote God's kingdom here on Earth now, not to withdraw from the world while awaiting the apocalypse and their heavenly rewards.

My studies challenged me to ask questions about how Christian America was. I wondered, If the kingdom of God was to be realized in America today, what would our institutions and politics look like?

Late afternoons and evenings, I studied with some of the leading thinkers at the University of Pennsylvania and Temple University, thanks to Eastern's scholarship arrangement with those schools. I earned a PhD in sociology from Temple and would use the tools of sociology to inform my theology from then on. I constantly worked to reconcile the two. I really felt that sociology raised all the right questions and theology provided all the right answers.

Every society creates a god for itself to legitimize its structures, rules, and regulations. When our nation goes to war, it's our societal god that lets us believe we are on God's side. Sociology critiques our culturally created gods and totems, which is a good thing for Christians. We have got to get rid of our false gods to worship the true God.

During the years I served as a pastor, my theology was focused on practical application. My job was to help people understand the faith, apply it to their lives, and grow in their love for God and their neighbors. My sermons were focused on spiritual matters, and whenever I mentioned social issues such as racism or the war in Vietnam, I felt the inevitable blowback from members who felt I was going "pink," or communist. But as a graduate student, I was free to explore a host of issues that aroused my curiosity and captured my imagination. Among them were the following:

Sociology of the family. Some of the first classes I took exposed me to research into family structures and functions that helped me see my own family in a brand-new light. I thought the Campolo family was unique in every way, but my studies showed us to be a typical representation of the American immigrant underclass experience.

I also studied empirical research that made it pretty clear that sexual orientation is established at a very early stage in the psychosocial development of children, with most gay people realizing they experience same-sex attraction during childhood. I would remember this scientific research years later when the AIDS crisis broke out and my fellow evangelicals began claiming that the disease revealed God's judgment against gay people for choosing to be gay. I remain convinced that classes in sociology of the family should be required for every pastor and Christian counselor.

Sociology of religion. People like to think that their religious beliefs and practices are divinely ordained, but upon closer study the sociologist can see that many religious behaviors reflect social factors. For example, the hunger for social status can lead people to affiliate with churches they think will enhance that status.

As someone deeply committed to following Jesus and obeying the Bible, I was glad to see some of my nonbiblical sacred cows quickly fall by the wayside. It was eye-opening to see how social factors I did not understand had played a role in my beliefs and practices.

Professors introduced me to great books, including *The True Believer* by Eric Hoffer, which explained how mass movements arise. For years, this little book would be my sociological guide to the civil rights movement and opposition to the Vietnam War.

I also had the chance to do an up-close study of one of the many new "cults" that were emerging across America. Sociologists now avoid the word *cult*, favoring the less pejorative phrase "new religious movement." But I was able to gain a firsthand look at the cultic practices that groups use, as well as the mindsets of true believers who are willing to cut off all contact with their families or give all their possessions to a guru they may have met just a few weeks earlier. My research on cults, which were growing more popular, led to speaking engagements with church and social groups. Years later, when Lisa was in college, we went on a research trip together, spending a long weekend at a sleep-deprived retreat hosted by Sun Myung Moon's Unification Church, which used many cultic practices.

Theology. I had grown up within two fundamentalist branches of the Christian family: fundamentalist Baptists (who feared the world but did not let that stop them from loving and evangelizing their neighbors) and independent fundamentalists like the Bible Buzzards (who taught that the world is destined for hell and the way to live is to go overseas as a missionary to save the lost).

Theology classes opened new worlds for me and showed me that there is no such thing as an off-limits question in theology. I saw that Christian thinkers down through the ages had addressed pretty much every problem or question anyone could raise.

During my years as a pastor, I had no time for deep theological reflection, but had to do "theology on the run" in stolen moments here and there. Now, at seminary, my hungry mind was free to devour the works of Søren Kierkegaard, Karl Barth, Paul Tillich, and other provocative Christian thinkers. In addition to the specific lessons I learned from each theologian,

I was learning to think theologically, which I would apply to all manner of issues in the coming years.

Church history. Most Christians know a little bit about the church they attend but next to nothing about the many other Christian denominations and traditions that make up Christ's global body. At seminary, I learned how Christians decided which books would be included in the New Testament, created creeds to summarize their beliefs, and worked to articulate the complex doctrines we now embrace.

I was grateful to learn more about Catholic and Orthodox traditions that I had been raised to consider suspect. I also gained a better sense of how Protestants moved from the Reformation to a new era, featuring untold numbers of different denominations, as well as megachurches that in many ways seem to serve as their own mini-denominations. It was good to see where Baptist churches fit into God's plan.

Having grown up in a family of ex-Catholics, I was surprised to find that my study of Catholic history attracted me to the church. In the Catholic Church I saw an answer to the problem of authority. The pope speaks for God to the entire church, while Protestants are divided into many distinct tribes with no unifying voice on earth. The pope's authority is a powerful antidote to the multiple subjective interpretations of Scripture and doctrine that seem to plague Protestantism. In the Baptist tradition, it seemed as if every individual was an authority unto himself.

This problem of authority is inherent in the Protestant Reformation. Once each person is entitled to interpret Scripture individually, the resulting lack of authority leads to subjectivity and mass confusion. I saw the papal authority in the Catholic Church as a powerful antidote to the subjectivity I witnessed in Christian fundamentalists and in liberal "God is Dead" theologians. I have seen many evangelicals convert to Catholicism and Orthodoxy in an effort to address the problem of authority within evangelicalism.

Karl Marx's sociology. Growing up amid the anticommunist hysteria of the 1940s and 1950s, I heard that communism was evil and Karl Marx was satanic. But my father, who worked as a poorly paid immigrant laborer, had such a deep sympathy for labor movements that some considered him a socialist.

Studying Marx, I learned that behind the socialist revolutionary was a brilliant sociologist, whose pioneering insights revealed the powerful role economic systems play in shaping the historical development of nations.

Some critics have wrongly claimed that I am a communist. I am not. Nor do I embrace Marx's dialectical materialist philosophy. I am a Christian sociologist who was deeply challenged by the social observations and analysis Marx offered in *Das Kapital.* As I studied Marx's descriptions of the tensions between poor, oppressed people and rich, powerful people, I thought about how Jesus repeatedly identified with and ministered to the poor and the oppressed people of his day.

Secularism. Years before the cover of *Time* asked, "Is God Dead?" I had the pleasure to study with Paul van Buren, a renowned theologian. Those familiar with his work might wonder how I could associate with someone linked to "God is Dead" theology. But sociology was central to van Buren's focus on "secular Christianity," a concept later spread further in *The Secular City* by Harvey Cox.

I did not agree with these thinkers' theology, but sixty-five years ago, they were prophetic in their social analysis. They saw then that secularism was for real and would be a growing influence in American culture.

Paul van Buren was an ordained Episcopal priest and professor of religion at Temple University, where I took classes as part of my sociology studies. He respected my conservative evangelical theology and helped me tailor my studies so that I could research how secularism affected the evangelical calling to evangelize nonbelievers. I will always appreciate the ways this "secular theologian" helped me develop my theology of secularism.

Einstein, Time, Space, and Eternity

Einstein's general theory of relativity, published in 1915, is now the accepted science of gravity in physics. I was able to meet Einstein when I was a high-school science student, and that experience had a lasting effect on my mind, my imagination, and my theology.

I wanted to explore how Einstein's theories intersected with the Bible's teaching on time and eternity. The result was *A Study of the Concept of Time in Contemporary Theology*, my 1961 master's thesis at Eastern Seminary. This was my thesis statement: "The description of time as a steady, everlasting, inexorable flow, streaming from the infinite past into the infinite future, and possessing a reality apart from man or his cosmos, is outdated and erroneous."

Einstein said that everything in the universe exists within four dimensions of space-time, and that really big objects—like our Sun—cause space-time to warp, affecting smaller objects—like our Earth—and distorting the way people on Earth experience space and time.

I explored how his ideas relate to biblical ideas about time, death, and the afterlife. I argued that both theologians and ordinary Christians should understand but not put their total faith in Einstein's theories, which have so far largely proven true. Why not? Christians should "date" various cosmological theories rather than "marrying" one and staying committed forever because science and scientific interpretations constantly develop and change.

Even though Einstein's theories underlie the accepted science of gravity today, future Einsteins will make new and further discoveries that will deepen and may even dramatically reshape our current understanding. That's how science works. Sometimes, as questing minds pursue a clear understanding of the world, false theories are perceived as true for a while. At other times, the truth is first misperceived as error before it is ultimately recognized and accepted.

Long ago, people believed that the Sun orbited the Earth, and such ideas found their way into the Bible. But Copernicus, a Christian, reasoned that the Earth actually orbited the Sun, and later Galileo proved this with his powerful new telescope. Scientists and theologians adapted to these new discoveries (but not before Galileo was charged with heresy for disagreeing with Scripture). There is a relentless human drive to understand the world and our place in it.

For me, this quest for understanding is ultimately theological. I am fascinated by the potential for science to help illuminate a better understanding of God's creation and his plan for us. In my master's thesis, I used Einstein's insights to explore a handful of seemingly confusing Bible passages, including God's statement to Moses that "I AM WHO I AM" (Exod. 3:14) and Christ's declaration that "Before Abraham was born, I am" (John 8:58). I concluded that eternity is not something we will experience later, but is here and now.

I believe that God has given us two books to study—the book of Scripture, which contains his revelation to us, and the book of nature, which science helps us understand. The Bible teaches that God created everything, while science explains how he did it. We run into trouble when we try to force the Bible to answer the how questions, or use science to answer the why questions. I believe in the faith-affirming role of science, even as I recognize the existence of religious truths and mysteries that our imperfect knowledge still cannot account for or explain.

Eastern is a pro-science school that requires all students to take basic science classes and is one of the few Christian schools with its own astronomical observatory. Eastern students understand what the psalmist meant when he wrote: "The heavens declare the glory of God; the skies proclaim the work of his hands" (Ps. 19:1). They share David's sense of awe and wonder at all that God has made.

It's too bad that some "young Earth" Christians reject science and instead believe that everything was created less than ten thousand years ago—a notion that is growing harder to believe and defend now that the James Webb Space Telescope is revealing images of light from stars that are billions of years old. Unlike everything else in our cosmos, God always was, always will be, and always is. As I argued in my paper, God lives in an eternal now.

Einstein believed in a hidden force that helped create the Earth, but he never called that force by the name of God. One day I asked the brilliant architect, systems theorist, and philosopher Buckminster Fuller about that. Fuller, the man who gave us geodesic domes and the concept of "Spaceship Earth," taught in the University of Pennsylvania's sociology department at the time. When I asked him if he would call the universe's hidden force God, he did not help me much.

"Call it anything you want," he said.

I concluded that this is one of the places where God's revelation can fill in the blanks that science cannot answer.

An Author Is Born

My theology/sociology double vision helped me write my first book, *A Denomination Looks at Itself*, a 1971 project commissioned by the American Baptists, who had recently moved their denominational headquarters to nearby Valley Forge, Pennsylvania. The American Baptists hired a polling firm to find out what church members thought about the denomination they were part of. After the polling firm delivered its report, denominational officials asked me to use my background in theology and sociology to interpret the data and explore some of the ways we could respond to the report. The resulting book was released by the denomination's publishing house.

My preface, which includes a thank-you to Paul van Buren, reflects my double-vision approach: "It is essential for the Christian to understand which aspects of his faith are cultural representations and which transcend the culture and have eternal moorings. With such discernment he will be able to free himself from the idolatrous tendency to worship the products of his culture as though they were God ordained." Looking back now, I can see that the language I used, which was a reflection of my culture, was not sufficiently inclusive of all Christian believers, not just men.

In the pages that followed, I took a closer look at the million and a half people who considered themselves American Baptists: they were upper middle class, more highly educated than the average American, and more comfortable with formal church. They were more at home with upwardly mobile Presbyterians than Pentecostal Christians.

I also dealt with the fact that our denomination had a higher median age than the population at large. We were an older person's church, which comes with consequences, as I explained: "The youth are underrepresented in the membership of all major denominations. This may be because religion tends to serve a supportive function for the socioeconomic system with which young people seem increasingly disenchanted. . . . Religious institutions which are identified with a social establishment that is increasingly under attack by the prophets of the youth culture (Pete Seeger, Bob Dylan, and Joan Baez) can hardly gain in popularity within this segment of the population."

I also explored discrimination against women. "It may not be surprising to learn that 63% of American Baptists are women, (but) while females are the majority of the membership of the denomination . . . they represent a definite minority on the policy-making committees and among the executives and elected officials." Unless something changed quickly, the denomination was doomed to extinction, a conclusion reached by many mainline denominations.

My first book was neither beautifully written nor a bestseller, but it fulfilled its purpose by helping our denominational leaders better understand some of the challenges they faced. The book would be used for years at Denver Seminary and other schools.

My writing style may have been overly academic, but that was because academic papers were the only thing I knew how to write. It would have surprised me then to know how many opportunities to develop a more accessible writing style would later come my way.

CHAPTER 14

TEACHING THE QUEST GENERATION

"Good teachers are good learners," one of my professors said. If so, I must have been a great teacher. It was 1964, and I was teaching sociology by day at Eastern University and taking courses by night at the University of Pennsylvania, for credit toward my doctorate at Temple University.

As a student, I was wrestling with important philosophical and sociological ideas. As a teacher, I was interacting with bright and passionate young people who were on a mission to discover themselves, uncover the meaning of life, and figure out ways to change the world for the better.

Studying sociology opened new intellectual vistas, helped me understand social relationships in ways I had never considered before, and constantly challenged me to develop biblical and theologically sound responses to the many social problems Americans face.

Not long after I started teaching, it became clear that lecturing and engaging students was exactly what I should be doing, and standing behind a classroom lectern was exactly where I should be doing it. I loved the intellectual and spiritual back-and-forth with students. Teaching would be my new ministry, and students seemed to find me interesting enough that my classes started filling up until they overflowed.

I was able to serve in a pastoral role at Eastern by working as the campus chaplain. My job description included finding speakers for our chapel services, speaking in classes about integrating faith with knowledge, and counseling students who came to my office with questions or problems.

I remember bringing in many speakers who combined faith with social action. William Sloane Coffin was a liberal Protestant thinker who was the chaplain at Yale and an outspoken critic of America's war in Vietnam. The Reverend Leon Sullivan was a nationally known civil rights leader who started the Opportunities Industrialization Center—OIC—in Philadelphia in 1964, which was based in a defunct jail. He fought racial discrimination in jobs and hiring by offering vocational, educational, and life-skills training to Black people.

I suspect my old friends in the Bible Buzzards looked at the 1960s as a horrible time of social disruption, sexual revolution, widespread use of drugs, and cultic religions. It's true that there was much about the era that was destructive. But I saw another side to the Sixties, as a glorious time of unprecedented opportunity for the church to speak to a generation of seekers engaged on a vast personal and spiritual quest.

My Eastern students expected me to apply Christian principles to everything we discussed in the classroom, and their pointed questions kept me on my toes. I would often seek out my seminary professors to learn their insights about the complex issues raised by my college students.

A Christian Professor at a Secular School

I was still completing my PhD at Temple in 1965 when the University of Pennsylvania asked me to teach sociology classes there. My Penn students—who included Jewish intellectuals and lesbian feminists—had not signed up for the faith-based lectures I gave at Eastern, but for a secular college course on sociology, yet they still asked questions about my faith.

I told my students up front that I had served as a pastor and was teaching at Eastern. They immediately peppered me with questions about theology, religious hypocrisy, and why Christians who follow Jesus, the Prince of Peace, seem to prefer war. This was more than a merely intellectual question for the male students, who feared that they might soon be compelled to fight in Vietnam.

In class, students would often ask, "So, what do Christians believe about social change today?" and other open-ended questions. I was pleasantly surprised that many students found ways to ask me about my faith in my office or during gatherings of students after class. One group would join me on Thursday nights after our evening class. The talks could go on until midnight or longer. I did not want to preach, so I adapted Jesus's model of asking deep, probing questions that laid bare people's unquestioned beliefs or biases.

It was a joy for me to work and serve Jesus at a secular university amid the young men and women who were part of this questing generation. At Penn as well as at Eastern, students and I spent hours discussing the sociological trends that were reshaping America, as well as critiquing the establishment church and the answers it was offering to the challenges of war, race, poverty, nuclear weapons, and humanity's role in space.

We also had heated discussions on books by provocative authors such as Vance Packard, a Penn alumnus, whether it was his look at the psychological and emotional tricks played by the advertising industry (1957's *The Hidden Persuaders*); Americans' fascination with social rank and the desperate things we will do to achieve it (1959's *The Status Seekers*); "planned obsolescence," in which corporations sell us more stuff by making regular superficial changes, like automakers do with their annual new models (1960's *The Waste Makers*); or corporate executives, their structured lives, and their need for conformity (1962's *The Pyramid Climbers*).

We also debated Charles Reich's *The Greening of America*, which claimed the emerging counterculture embraced Consciousness III, a fundamental intellectual shift from previous generations that embraced personal freedom, egalitarianism, and recreational drugs. He helped me see where the young people were "coming from," as they said back then.

The more I interacted with students, the more I realized my professor was right. Good teachers do more than dispense information. They must also listen and absorb new information. Good teachers often learn as much or more from their students than their students learn from them. That was certainly the case for me, as hundreds of young men and women shared with me their thoughts, dreams for the future, fears about the challenges of life, and the spiritual answers they relied on.

The Search for Self

In the 1960s, America was facing a generation gap that pitted a new generation of young people who wanted to change the world against older establishment adults who preferred the status quo. Most of the time I felt as if I was in the middle of that yawning gap. I heard people on both sides questioning and complaining about the people on the other side.

No subject was out of bounds in my faculty offices at Eastern and Penn. Students talked to me about war and peace, religion and spirituality, the individual and society, racial divisions, sexual tensions, faith and doubt, communism and capitalism, and the politics of groups like Students for a Democratic Society. I also started learning about feminism and homosexuality, two new subjects that I had not heard much about at Eastern.

The subject that got the most attention was the quest for a personal identity, an authentic self, a fully "actualized" life. Everything had to be real, not plastic. Everything needed to come from within, not from external forces or other people's expectations. "I've got to find myself," students told me, repeatedly.

Another student put it this way: "I'm tired of playing the role that my family has prescribed for me, that school has prescribed for me, that church has prescribed for me, or that society has prescribed for me. I need to be me."

One student told me he saw the quest for personal identity as something like peeling an onion. "I want to peel away each outer layer of the onion like I'm peeling away each of the roles that have come to define me. But what happens if after peeling everything away I discover that there's nothing there, and I'm nothing more than the sum total of these socially prescribed identities?"

Underneath this intense personal quest, I saw a deep spiritual quest. Many long-haired hippie students at Penn interrogated me at length about Christianity, even if they were seeking answers in Buddhism, Hinduism, or a newly christened guru on campus. Some students had developed critiques of Christianity that led them to turn their backs on the Bible and embrace one or more of the burgeoning non-Christian religious movements, including newfangled cults that used authoritarian methods to keep disciples under control. I was sad to see how a sincere search for healing and salvation could result in spiritual, psychological, financial, or even sexual abuse.

Penn would soon send me on the road to do presentations about new religious movements for parents who were confused about why young people left churches and joined cults. This experience gave me a preview of the public speaking I would enjoy later in my career.

"Personal identities are not waiting to be discovered through introspection, but are determined by our commitments," I told worried parents. "And I'm afraid that the church has failed to call this generation to a radical commitment to God. If the church loses this generation of young people, it will not be because we asked them to commit too much, but because we asked them to commit too little."

My work led to occasional television appearances on *The Mike Douglas Show*, where the host would drill me about issues concerning young people in our society. I felt ready and eager to discuss just about any question that would come my way. This led to further invitations to appear on other television shows.

When I was not spending my time on campus with students, I would often hear conservative Christians from older generations dismiss the quest generation as a bunch of privileged, self-absorbed navel-gazers. "Why don't they grow up, cut their hair, get a job, and settle down? That's where they will find their identity!"

But in my role as a teacher, I had greater access to these young people, and that familiarity gave me more understanding and love. I admired my students for wrestling sincerely with life's important questions like "Who am I?" and "What am I supposed to do?"

I tried to tell critical adults to take a deeper look and to search within their hearts to find a capacity for greater empathy and appreciation. "Young people are giving us a golden opportunity to listen, understand their challenges, and offer ways that the Christian faith has the answers they are seeking," I said. "These students are telling me that what we experience is more important than what we know, that who we are is more important than what we have, that who we are is determined by our commitments rather than our social achievements. Are they wrong for wanting to live by these ideals?"

As a college professor, it was my job to teach and share my knowledge with young people. I did my best to fulfill those responsibilities, and I hope I was effective. As I look back on my teaching career, however, I can see that I received as much or more than I shared in my interactions with my students. The student talks I had in my office changed my attitudes, my teaching, and my preaching. The provocative questions these students asked me would inform many of the books I would later write.

Teaching and Learning

I taught the basic "Introduction to Sociology" course at Penn from 1965 to 1975, and my classes grew larger and larger each semester. In time, I had classes of hundreds of students in the

Irvine Auditorium, a huge lecture hall. The sociology department provided me with a team of graduate assistants who took attendance, graded student papers, and offered makeup tests, to relieve me of these duties.

Eventually I worked with a crew of ten graduate assistants who made my life incredibly easy. All I had to do was show up and lecture, which I loved. My years of preaching experience paid off, and my assistants gave me the time and help I needed to make each lecture as interesting and engaging as possible.

As we worked together, my graduate assistants and I enjoyed lengthy, deep conversations that explored new areas I had not heard much about at Eastern. Many of my assistants were liberal-minded women, so I received a crash course in the women's liberation movement and feminism. I remember talking about Betty Friedan's 1963 book, *The Feminine Mystique*, which addressed women's efforts to find personal fulfillment outside their traditional roles as housewives and mothers. These talks were the first time I realized what the women's movement was really all about.

Before I got to know these assistants, I had thought of myself as a decent guy who was plenty respectful—even chivalrous—to members of the opposite sex. But as these highly educated women regularly informed me, I still had a lot of work to do. My female graduate assistants routinely alerted me to the all-too-frequent demonstrations of my sexism and male bias, which had previously been invisible to me.

What an education! I learned that I needed to watch my words and be on the lookout for sexist overtones or attitudes. I am still a work in progress, and deeply ingrained assumptions and patterns of thought and speech are hard to break. Still, I will be forever grateful for the eye-opening education that these bright young women gave me and for the change in my perspective that followed.

I also witnessed to my assistants about Jesus, and just as Jesus said in his parable of the sower and the seed, some of my mini-sermons were welcomed, while others fell on stony ground. One day at lunch with two of my female graduate assistants, I asked them what they thought about something Jesus said about the issue we were discussing. My question brought a response I was not expecting.

"Your religion leaves much to be desired," one of them told me. "You're so sure of yourself, like you've got everything all wrapped up in a nice, neat package, like you have all the answers."

The more she talked, the more I could see that she was right. Over the years I had developed the habit of hearing the first few words of a student's comments and then quickly working on a clever response, often recycling answers I had worked out while talking to other students. Some students felt I was employing my theology like a kind of cannon, blasting away at their objections instead of listening and really understanding what they were saying. They were right. I tried to learn to be a better listener.

Homosexuality 101

My interactions with students also began my learning about homosexuality. This was a relatively new topic for me. I had never heard it addressed in churches or at Eastern College or Seminary, but had learned a bit about the topic in the sociology of the family classes I took at Penn.

One Penn student was a gay man who was involved in a long-term relationship he called a marriage in the days before same-sex marriage became legal. This man became a very close friend, and I got to know both him and his partner quite well. I thought they were great guys who made a wonderful couple. People who knew them asked them for dating advice.

I was also learning about homophobia. I told myself and others that I was not homophobic, but upon deeper reflection I realized that was not really true. I thought back to my high-school days and my weak response to a group of boys who mercilessly picked on the school's one openly gay student, a boy I will call Roger. Roger was routinely picked on and humiliated by a group of school bullies who seemed to delight in taunting him.

I wanted to stand up for Roger and challenge the boys who picked on him, and at times I spoke up on his behalf. But I did not do so nearly as often or as forcefully as I should have. I am ashamed to say that I was stopped by cowardice, politics, and a selfish concern for my reputation. Instead of doing what was right, I bowed to peer pressure and looked the other way when confronted with injustice. My shame in having done so has haunted me for decades, as it should.

Decades later, at the peak of the deadly AIDS crisis, I watched and listened as evangelicals relentlessly condemned gays and even suggested that they deserved the scourge of a deadly disease as a punishment for engaging in homosexual behavior. I acknowledge that, once again, I failed to speak out as I should have, to insist on the fair and humane treatment of gay people, who were created by God just like straight people and deserve love and respect, especially during times of sickness and great suffering. Once again, I was ashamed of my weak response and promised to do better in the future. My later efforts to honor that promise would eventually bring me into conflict with evangelical leaders.

Faith into Action

I thought I had left pastoral work behind when I stormed out of that horrible meeting at Upper Merion Baptist Church, but my days as a pastor were not yet over. I was invited to be interim pastor at First Baptist Church of Trenton, New Jersey, in 1964. I jumped at the chance because I really missed preaching the gospel and I wanted to serve the local community.

First Baptist was only a few hundred yards away from the Trenton Boys Club. One day leaders of the club approached me and shared their concerns about underprivileged kids in the neighborhood who were struggling in school.

"Can the church do anything to help our kids?" they asked me.

I immediately saw the possibility of recruiting Eastern students to come to the Boys Club and provide tutoring on Saturdays. Before long, some of my Eastern students were making the weekly one-hour journey to Trenton to offer academic support to nearly one hundred boys and girls.

Word spread, and soon other communities were asking for similar help. I told them all that I would try to round up more students so we could establish tutoring programs. We did so in South Philadelphia, with Lutheran pastor John Cochran. We did so in Camden, New Jersey, with Rosedale Baptist Church and Hope Baptist Church. And we did so at a troubled high-rise government housing project called Southwark in Philadelphia. By the 1970s, two hundred Eastern students were dedicating their time to serving the needs of these communities.

Not everyone at Eastern was happy about this development. Some worried that the school's vans would have their windows broken while parked in poor urban areas. Others complained that these service programs, which were not part of the college's curriculum, distracted from the school's academic emphasis.

But soon, service projects *would* be made part of the curriculum at Eastern, and in time, they became a hallmark of an Eastern education. Now, sixty years later, every undergraduate student participates in some form of community service in poor neighborhoods. This experience has shaped the ministries of hundreds of Eastern graduates who have become Christian servants and leaders, including Shane Claiborne and Jonathan Wilson-Hartgrove.

This is how we put our faith into action at Eastern, and it changed our lives, the lives of the people we served, and the path Eastern would take in coming decades.

CHAPTER 15

FOLLOWING THE PRINCE OF PEACE IN A TIME OF WAR

The war in Vietnam began in 1955, but it remained mostly in the back of my mind until I began teaching students whose brothers and cousins and boyfriends were among the more than two million young men who would be drafted to fight—and possibly die—in this unpopular and ultimately unsuccessful conflict.

After President Lyndon Johnson escalated US troop numbers and bombings in 1965, college campuses across the country began to ring with chants of "Hey, hey, LBJ, how many kids did you kill today?"

At colleges like the University of California, Berkeley, and Columbia University in New York, large anti-war movements erupted. Students held massive rallies that nearly shut down campuses, and some students occupied administration buildings. In some cases, demonstrations turned violent and led to students burning buildings. This behavior would lead presidential candidate Richard Nixon to campaign on a platform that targeted unruly students.

Soon enough, more of my students at Penn would join the anti-war movement, bringing passionate discussions about war and peace, militarism and pacifism, to my classrooms and our after-class discussions. I was ready for the tumult because I had already thought long and hard about the ethics and morality of taking up arms to kill others.

WWJD?

I was still in high school when I got the letter telling me to visit the Selective Service office in Philadelphia and register for the draft. The Korean War was then in full swing. The timing was interesting. I had been reading a book called *In His Steps* by Charles Sheldon, a Congregationalist minister. The book encouraged Christians to walk in the footsteps of Jesus. That's what I wanted to do with my life. Sheldon wrote that when followers of Christ are weighing an important decision, they should ask themselves one simple question: "What would Jesus do?"

It seemed clear to me what Jesus would do about war based on his teaching in his Sermon on the Mount: "You have heard that it was said, 'Eye for eye, and tooth for tooth.' But I tell you, do not resist an evil person. If anyone slaps you on the right cheek, turn to them the other cheek also" (Matt. 5:38–39).

While Jesus never taught on the ethics of military service, there was one time when he made it clear that he opposed the use of weapons as a way of settling disputes. The scene happens after Jesus's Last Supper and before his crucifixion. Jesus is with his disciples at Gethsemane when Judas shows up, accompanied by "a large crowd armed with swords and clubs" (Matt. 26:47). As Matthew's Gospel tells us, "Then the men stepped forward, seized Jesus and arrested him. With that, one of Jesus' companions reached for his sword, drew it out and struck the servant of the high priest, cutting off his ear. 'Put your sword back in its place,' Jesus said to him, 'for all who draw the sword will die by the sword'" (Matt. 26:50–52).

This is what I was thinking about when I went to meet the Selective Service officer, who asked me, "Son, do you have any problems with serving your country's military?"

"Actually, I do have a problem," I told him. "I've just read this book called *In His Steps*, which teaches that to be a Christian you have to do what Jesus would do in any given situation. I can't imagine Jesus shoving a bayonet into someone's body and spilling their guts."

"You're making it sound very ugly," said the young lieutenant.

"Of course, it is ugly!" I said.

Unlike the many hawks, I was a follower of the Prince of Peace, and I sided with the Christian tradition of just-war theory. I believed the horrors and destruction of war should be turned to only as a last resort, not as a routine weapon of foreign policy. I did not believe the Korean War was just, and as a follower of Jesus I felt I could not fight in it.

Seeking to change course, the officer posed another challenge.

"Well, suppose you're in the Air Force. Could you drop a bomb on a village?"

"What do you think?" I asked the officer. "What should I do if I'm flying over an enemy village with an order to release the bombs and I pray, 'Jesus, if you were in my place, would you drop this bomb on this village?'"

"That's the dumbest thing I've ever heard," said the officer. "Jesus would never do that."

"Well then, that settles it for me, sir."

I wound up being classified as Class 4-F: "Registrant not qualified for military service." It was a very fair and accurate classification.

"What Are You Going to Do?"

A decade later, my Penn students were facing a similar dilemma as the Vietnam War draft carried on. Nearly all of them were against the war, and they routinely invited me to participate with them in their campaigns, marches, and protests designed to bring our boys back home.

By 1967, the anti-war movement had grown more popular nationwide. At Penn, anger over the war focused on the role the college played in conducting research on chemical warfare for the US government. It was rumored that Penn researchers had helped create the substances that caused so much destruction and pain in Vietnam. This meant that student tuition and fees were going to support some of the most inhumane aspects of the war.

Some Penn students burned their draft cards. Others protested when recruiters from the CIA and Dow Chemical Company, which made napalm, came to campus to interview students for jobs. Other students entertained acts of violence, such as attacking draft board offices, burning campus buildings, or conducting demonstrations at military facilities.

When leaders of Penn's anti-war movement confronted me, they demanded to know what I was going to do to help the cause. I was totally opposed to war, but also opposed to violent anti-war protests, so I came up with a more peaceful proposal.

"Why don't we organize a prayer vigil?" I asked, thinking this would be a wonderful opportunity for me to show the importance of my Christian faith in addressing one of the most pressing social issues of the time.

These activists had never considered anything like this, but as we talked about it they gradually warmed to the idea. I made it an ecumenical gathering by inviting a rabbi, an imam, and a Buddhist who was popular on campus.

When it came time for our vigil, hundreds of students gathered on the grass in front of the university library on a beautiful fall afternoon. After some brief comments and prayers from the religious leaders, we split people into groups so they could talk and pray in smaller gatherings of like-minded students. After a few hours, everybody left. The next day the vigil was front-page news in local papers, but that was not the end of it.

Soon, an art professor named Robert Engman and a group of eight fine arts students decided to commemorate the vigil and honor those who had died in the war by creating a big, stainless-steel peace symbol sculpture and placing it in the area of the gathering. The sculpture was later raised on a pole so it would be more visible across the campus.

Erected in 1967, that peace symbol still stands on the campus, near the entrance to the Van Pelt Library, as a quiet reminder of those turbulent times. Over the years, students seeking to address the issues of their day have returned to this spot to make their case.

Students at Eastern were not immune to the currents of the youth subculture, and about 150 Eastern students participated in a peace march against the war. The march picked up another fifty students from other schools by the time it reached the destination, a Quaker meeting house. Quakers are peace-loving Christians who founded the colony of Pennsylvania. The president of Haverford College, a nearby Quaker school, gave a talk about the Quaker tradition of pacifism and the role Quakers played in abolishing slavery and promoting women's rights. It was thrilling to see the peace movement meet Quaker pacifists whose ancestors came to these shores in the 1650s.

A "Laboratory" for the Evangelical Left

My Christian students at Eastern were more divided about the war. Some students followed my approach of asking, "What would Jesus do?" (This question eventually led to the development of the Red Letter Christians movement, which calls on believers to do precisely what Jesus called us to do; the name of the movement refers to the fact that some Bibles highlight Jesus's words in red print.) Other students came from families that taught that military service was next to godliness, that war was a necessary evil, that the anti-war peace sign was the "symbol of the American chicken," and that pacifists like me were part of the problem.

Students at America's Christian colleges were less caught up than their secular counterparts in the anti-war movement. That was because of numerous factors, including the tendency of Christians to support politicians who were more hawkish, and the feeling of some students that they should avoid debates about worldly political issues.

I encountered such resistance to anti-war sentiments in 1987, when I spoke at a huge student missions conference sponsored by a major Christian fellowship organization. In my talk, I described my meeting with the draft board officer. Students cheered, but the event organizers were shocked and angered. They later determined that they would not invite me to speak at that conference again. To them, I was unwisely engaging in unpalatable radical politics at a Christian event. But as I saw it, I was simply doing my best to preach the gospel and follow the teachings of Jesus, as I understood them.

I also worked with Ron Sider, a professor at Eastern Seminary who wrote the bestselling book *Rich Christians in an Age of Hunger* and led the organization Evangelicals for Social Action. Ron and I, along with Jim Wallis of Sojourners and Gordon Cosby of Church of the Saviour in Washington, DC, gathered a handful of students to stage a protest in the US Capitol rotunda. We knew we would be arrested for doing so, but we wanted to send a message to Congress that it should spend less on the military and more on services to meet the needs of the poor. We called authorities at the Capitol ahead of time to say we were coming. Once we arrived, a police officer approached us and said we would be arrested.

"We know," we said.

"But since we approve of what you're doing, we're going to arrest you very slowly, one at a time, so it will take all afternoon," the officer told us.

We went to jail very slowly, singing hymns along the way. While in jail, I had a fascinating discussion about whether Jesus was the messiah with a rabbi who joined us for the protest.

It was not too long after these events that Eastern added *justice* to its motto. Today that motto reads: "Eastern University is a diverse, Christ-centered community preparing graduates to impact the world through faith, reason, and justice."

Back in the classroom, I challenged my students to base their opinions about war and peace and everything else squarely on Jesus's ministry and teaching. I challenged them to come up with a fully Christian theology that dealt with violence and war. Not all of them agreed with my position, but all seriously engaged the issue, seeking to apply their faith to this conundrum. I call myself a troubled pacifist because I recognize I would not have the opportunity to advocate peace and nonviolence if it had not been for the actions of the brave men and women in our military.

Over time, my approach to war and other ethical issues helped nudge Eastern toward a theologically conservative but socially progressive approach to the world's challenges. A 2021 article in *The Christian Century* took a look at the college's unique role. The headline told the story: EASTERN UNIVERSITY HAS SERVED AS THE EVANGELICAL LEFT'S LABORATORY.[1]

The article described how Eastern students such as Shane Claiborne and Jonathan Wilson-Hartgrove have become leaders of organizations focused on social justice, racial equality, care for the poor, and opposition to warfare. "I think Eastern was well ahead of the curve on these social justice issues," historian John Fea said in the *Century*'s article. Looking back, I am proud that I was able to preach this stuff even when I took a lot of heat for it.

I could not have guessed then that there was another topic on which my public statements, in time, would generate even more heat and controversy. As time went on, I was forced as never before to deal with issues of sexuality.

CHAPTER 16

CONFRONTING SEXUALITY AND ABORTION

If you spend time around college students, you cannot avoid the topic of sex. That was especially true during the sexual revolution of the 1960s and 1970s, which shook up society, recast social norms, and led to disputes about birth control, abortion, and homosexuality—disputes that continue today.

As old rules were being cast off and new freedoms were being enjoyed, evangelicals were preparing to make concerns about these issues their primary public expression for the next half century. These battles would force me to rethink my approach to sexual morality and ethics, which would lead some conservative Christian leaders to brand me as a liberal or even, in some cases, a heretic.

Before and after *Roe*

Some of the saddest conversations I have ever had were with young people who suddenly found themselves dealing with an unplanned pregnancy. For many young Christians in this predicament, there is no good option, and oftentimes the sad dilemma is painfully compounded by the shame and fear of incurring the wrath of morally strict Christian parents, and by the prospect of being humiliated or even ostracized by a judgmental church community.

When counseling distraught young people in these circumstances, I have tried to focus first and foremost on the Christian principles of compassion, forgiveness, and reconciliation. Recognizing the enormity of the hard choices that face them, I have encouraged them to pray and to listen to God's voice, and then to reflect and talk about the choice they feel led to make and the reasons for that choice. A person in crisis needs to be assured of the steadfastness of God's love and reminded of the priceless gifts of forgiveness, redemption, and grace.

In our society, abortion has long been a deeply politicized issue, both despite and because of its profound religious, ethical, and moral dimensions. I have lived long enough to see our country take three different approaches to abortion. In broad strokes, I have seen abortion be treated as

- illegal in most states, in the days before the Supreme Court's 1973 decision in *Roe v. Wade*;
- constitutionally protected, with some limits, under *Roe*; and
- now illegal again in many states, since the Court overturned *Roe* in June 2022.

The Catholic Church has long and consistently opposed abortion, but the evangelical perspective has been more malleable over time. It took a while for evangelicals to come around to the strong anti-abortion stance that currently prevails in our community.

I use the term *anti-abortion* deliberately. I know that people who oppose abortion usually prefer to call themselves *pro-life*, but I think someone has to do more than oppose abortion in order to be truly pro-life. For example, a person who opposes abortion but approves of war, the death penalty, easy access to guns, and lax environmental standards is not really pro-life. Many churches claim they stand for life, but the fact of the matter is that Christian women get abortions at similar rates to nonbelievers.

What has led to the hardening of an anti-abortion perspective on abortion within the evangelical community? No doubt there are many contributing factors, but two stand out to me. In 1979, Francis Schaeffer and C. Everett Koop challenged evangelicals to make abortion their top political issue through their book and film *Whatever Happened to the Human Race?* Soon thereafter, *Christianity Today* magazine and groups like the Southern Baptist Convention revisited and began to revise their earlier support, or at least tolerance, for abortion in some cases.

Eventually, the abortion issue became a way for Republicans to lock in evangelical voters. In turn, the evangelical community's political clout and increasingly vocal anti-abortion perspective have affected Republican presidential appointments to the Supreme Court. The Court's decision to overturn *Roe*—thereby wiping out what had long been recognized as a constitutionally protected right—never would have happened without a half-century campaign led by committed Christian conservative activists and millions of evangelically minded laypeople.

Unpacking the Issues

Abortion involves many complex theological, biological, and legal issues, but most of the information we get from anti-abortion groups is simplified and politicized. Let's take a brief look at two underlying issues.

The anti-abortion movement is based on two major claims: the theological claim that human life begins at conception and the legal claim that abortion is murder and that the government has the authority to intervene if lives are in danger.

I do not want to be misunderstood. Although I consider myself pro-life in a sense—that is, in the broadest possible sense—I disagree with both of the anti-abortion movement's two foundational claims, about when life begins and who should decide whether a woman must carry a baby to term. Let me tell you why.

When does life begin? The Christian anti-abortion movement of the twentieth and twenty-first centuries is based on the theological claim that human life begins at conception. This claim has been the prevailing Christian position for centuries, but it is far from the only position on the issue, and today many mainline Protestant denominations take differing views. I agree with those who believe that the book of Exodus reflects ambiguity about fetal life: "When people who are fighting injure a pregnant woman so that there is a miscarriage, and yet no further harm follows, the one responsible shall be fined what the woman's husband demands, paying as much as the judges determine" (Exod. 21:22).

St. Augustine opposed abortion from the moment of conception, but he believed that "ensoulment"—the process of biological life taking in a soul—actually happens later. He taught that a man's sperm contains huge numbers of infinitesimal human beings, but most of these will never reach birth. My position on when an embryo becomes human takes a similar approach to Augustine's view on gradual ensoulment.

My conclusion is that human personhood does not begin at conception but develops gradually as the unborn child develops. All life is sacred, but in the very beginning, this new life is not yet fully human. Things change significantly after the first signs of a functioning brain and nervous system at around six to eight weeks after conception.

Humanness is not only biological, but also social and spiritual. For Christians, in the big picture, the process of becoming truly human takes a lifetime, incorporating language, self-awareness, moral values, a relationship with Jesus Christ, participation in a local church, and more.

I believe that in the womb the embryo becomes increasingly human as it develops a brain and interacts with the mother before birth. This is why I join with those who oppose late-term abortions.

I respect those who sincerely believe that human life begins at conception, and who therefore are compelled to believe that any abortion is murder. I share their distress that greater access to abortion after *Roe* has led many people to treat abortion as a form of birth control, resulting in more than fifty million abortions in the last half century.

This brief summary fails to address the complexity of the theological, biological, and legal issues involved in when life begins. This view can be debated, and believe me, it *has* been debated for millennia by Bible scholars, theologians, biologists, and ethicists. I continue to debate it, as we all should. I must confess that I now spend more time contemplating when life ends, which according to the medical experts happens when brain waves cease.

I have little sympathy for angry anti-abortion activists who claim they represent the only true Christian or godly position on the issue and that everyone who disagrees with them is evil. As in so many cases, love is preferable to condemnation amid disagreements with brothers and sisters in Christ.

I am also critical of pro-lifers who, in the words of former Congressman Barney Frank, "believe that life begins at conception and ends at birth" with regard to public policies that deliver needed help to poor and needy families. Many women seek abortions because they cannot afford a family. It seems that if people are truly pro-life, they would not only oppose abortion but also support both private charity and government programs that provide nutrition and care to both poor and needy mothers and their new babies.

Who should make decisions? I might understand matters differently if I lived in Afghanistan, where the Taliban controls public morality, but I'm a freedom-loving American who firmly believes:

- Adults decide what they do with their own bodies in bedrooms and hospital rooms—not judges, government officials, or leaders of politically active religious groups.
- Our laws should promote the common good, not impose the beliefs of a dedicated and effective minority on the entire population.

I'm also a committed Christian who is a strong feminist, as was Jesus, radically so for his day. It's sad to see restrictions on women's rights to personal autonomy and women's freedom to make basic decisions about their own bodies.

I reluctantly and ambivalently supported the freedom granted by *Roe v. Wade* because I have known women who became pregnant through rape, incest, or accident, and I believe they, and not a government policy or bureaucracy, should get to make the difficult decisions about what to do in those circumstances.

In July 2022, after the Supreme Court overturned *Roe* and more than a dozen states, including Ohio, outlawed all abortions, a ten-year-old Ohio girl became pregnant through rape and had to travel from her home state to Indiana, where abortion remained legal, to be spared from continuing trauma. Pro-life groups at first dismissed the story as a hoax, but in fact thousands of young girls become pregnant every year. Is it Christian and pro-life to pass laws that force traumatized and unprepared girls to give birth amid such tragedy? Likewise, is it Christian and pro-life to pass laws that force women, including mothers whose young children need them, to sacrifice their own lives, in some cases, in order to continue with pregnancies that their bodies simply cannot sustain?

I have some predictions for our post-*Roe* world, as follows:

- Confessing Christians will continue to have abortions at nearly the same rates as unbelievers.
- Many men will continue to evade responsibility for the consequences of their sexual behavior.
- More women will face daunting decisions and, in many states, will have less authority to choose their path.
- Women of means will travel to places where abortion remains legal, should they want a safe abortion and live in a state where they are prohibited. Poor women will be unable to do so.
- More women will be injured or die from unsafe abortion procedures.
- Women experiencing miscarriages may face greater danger, as well as legal jeopardy.
- More children will be born to women who do not want them, women who are not prepared to parent them, and women who lack the resources to care for them.
- Even after nearly half a century of anti-abortion activism, Christians will still not create the kind of support system of birth doctors, adoptive parents, and caregivers that many women facing unplanned pregnancies will need.
- And pro-family-values voters will continue to oppose social-safety-net programs that serve children after they leave their mothers' wombs.

Surely, we can do better.

Created Man and Woman

It seems that many of the most divisive culture-war issues involve sex and gender, and most of the big issues are wrapped up in complex questions of theology and law. Are women and men created equal? That's a theological and philosophical question. How should women and men be treated under the law? That's a legal and political question.

Americans have long debated the legal treatment of women, in light of the traditionally different roles of men and women in our society. As a result of the suffrage movement, women gained the right to vote in 1920, with the passage of the Nineteenth Amendment to the United States Constitution. Three years later, the first Equal Rights Amendment (ERA) was proposed in Congress with the goal of achieving full legal equality for women. The bill failed. A proposed Equal Rights Amendment was introduced in Congress once again in 1971. The proposed amendment was designed to make men and women equal before the law in owning property, obtaining a divorce, and having access to work.

The most powerful ERA opponent was Phyllis Schlafly, a conservative Catholic and loyal member of the John Birch Society. She claimed the ERA would hurt women and families. Soon pro-family groups like Focus on the Family agreed, claiming that if women were granted greater economic freedoms, fewer moms would stay home and raise children.

I favor the ERA and support full legal equality for women because I am convinced that Jesus was a radical feminist. In Jesus's day it was common to relegate women to inferior status, but the Bible makes clear that Jesus treated women as equals.

The apostle Paul also championed women, teaching, "There is neither Jew nor Gentile, neither slave nor free, nor is there male and female, for you are all one in Christ Jesus" (Gal. 3:28). Paul also taught that women should submit to their husbands (Eph. 5:22–25), but the kind of marriage Paul envisioned involves mutual submission of both husband and wife.

New Thinking on Sexual Orientation

The gay rights movement began after the 1969 Stonewall riots in protest of police arrests of gay men at New York City's Stonewall Inn. Conservative Christians soon signaled their opposition. Anita Bryant—a former Miss Oklahoma who had a string of Top 40 hit singles in the 1950s and 1960s—launched the first national attack on gay rights. "Homosexuals cannot reproduce, they must recruit," she warned, claiming that gays were coming after people's children.

Since then, opposition to gay rights has become a core creed of the evangelical movement. Pro-family groups, including Focus on the Family, have raised more than $100 million to target the "gay agenda." That money has done little to slow Americans' growing support for same-sex marriage, which is now at an all-time high, but it has succeeded in dividing churches, voters, and families over this issue.

In the last fifty years, my position on homosexuality and equal rights for all LGBTQ people has evolved. In fact, it has changed in some fundamental ways, and I no longer believe some of the things I used to believe. As a result, my views have been misunderstood by some and twisted by others seeking to silence me. Let me trace my shifting understanding on this topic.

What is homosexuality? I started in ignorance. Other than knowing a gay boy in high school, I knew next to nothing about homosexuality. In the 1950s, the subject was taboo. I heard no sermons about the dangers of the "gay agenda," and the sex education I received in public schools was boring, rudimentary, and inadequate to prepare young people for the challenges they face.

When I was a student at Eastern College and Seminary, my classes never addressed same-sex attraction. That's why I did not take my first serious look at the subject until I studied the sociology of the family at the University of Pennsylvania with Dr. William Kephart.

Scripture and biology. The few biblical passages addressing homosexuality condemn various forms of behavior. But the scant research available on homosexuality in the 1950s and 1960s, when I got my education, suggested:

- Nobody really knows what causes homosexuality.
- Homosexual orientation appears to be something that a percentage of people *have* or *are*, not something they *choose*.
- Many become aware that they are sexually different from others early in their social/psychological development, meaning they do not remember ever having an earlier, heterosexual identity.
- It's nearly impossible to change orientation once a person's sexual identity is established. This is the reason that most of the Christian ministries that once promoted "conversion therapy" have now closed or stopped offering it, and I support legislation outlawing this often-barbaric practice, which has been associated with far too many suicides.

Along with other Christian thinkers, I have tried to understand how biblical teaching addressed a new understanding of homosexuality that took orientation into account. After reading many scholars, I concluded that Paul's tough language in Romans 1:27 ("Men committed shameful acts with other men, and received in themselves the due penalty for their error") referred to sexual practices associated with idolatry and temple prostitution in the ancient world, not faithful gay or lesbian relationships. I also made a distinction between behavior (one has choices about how one behaves) and orientation (many gay people say they never chose to be gay).

Some Christian organizations have focused their attention on efforts to change homosexuals into heterosexuals through counseling and training. But experience has shown that the success of these efforts has been close to nil. These efforts have created many false hopes and caused much emotional and spiritual harm for men and women struggling with their sexual identities, even driving many to suicide.

AIDS and compassion. When the AIDS crisis blew up, evangelicalism's ugly homophobia problem came out of the closet.

Instead of showing compassion for the sick, the dying, and the bereaved, a number of high-profile and politically oriented Christian media stars have blamed gays for everything from tornadoes to 9/11. But I follow a Jesus who responded to the hurt and sorrow of others with love and compassion, not with judgmentalism and hate.

I deeply respected C. Everett Koop, whom I got to know through his son, one of my sociology students at Eastern. Koop served as the surgeon general of the United States at a time when our country was in the midst of the worst part of the AIDS crisis. Koop was condemned by many evangelicals for organizing and directing one of the biggest governmental mailings in our country's history, in order to educate Americans about AIDS. As I saw it, this was an act of compassion.

Of course, not all evangelicals responded to the AIDS crisis with hate and harsh judgment. Christian musician Steve Camp was one who took a different approach. He and I partnered together to create an organization called ACCT (AIDS Crisis and Christians Today) that sought to encourage Christians to extend the compassion of Jesus to people who suffered as a result of the AIDS scourge.

We invited Christian musicians to present songs they had written about the AIDS crisis, and they performed those songs in fundraising concerts in Nashville and Boston. Steve and three other writers—Rob Frazier, Kim Maxfield-Camp, and Phil McHugh—collaborated on the song "Do You Feel Their Pain?"

"We want pastors in the local church to take the lead in the emotional and spiritual and daily care of people with AIDS," Steve Camp said in a 1992 interview. "The government and other people are looking for support medically; we think the church should lead the way spiritually. And in issues of love and compassion and hope, not only to people with AIDS but also to their families."[2]

Steve Green's song "Rescue the Perishing" summed up our approach:

> Rescue the perishing,
> Care for the dying.
> Jesus is merciful,
> Jesus will save.

I was a longtime moral conservative. But unlike many evangelicals who condemned gay people and claimed AIDS was God's judgment on their sin, I believed Jesus commands us to love all our neighbors, whether they are gay or straight. Did that make me liberal? I did not think so.

When I sometimes spoke for large insurance-company gatherings, I became friends with Ronald D. Barbaro when he was the president of Prudential Insurance Company of America's Canadian operations. Barbaro helped develop living-need benefits in Canada, and he was the first president of an insurance company to apply these benefits to people diagnosed with AIDS. I considered this an example of the compassionate solutions people can find to difficult problems.

I saw another example of inspiring Christians to work compassionately for AIDS patients after I spoke at a chapel service at what is now Point Loma Nazarene University. During my talk, I spoke about the need to do something about the AIDS crisis in Southern California. Afterward, about two dozen students, including a nurse, came backstage to follow up. After some discussion, they decided to rent a house and set up a hospice for people who were dying of AIDS.

Months later, I was traveling through the San Diego airport and stopped at a newsstand, which was my habit during trips. Among the publications I saw, a newspaper for gays and lesbians caught my eye. On the front page was a photo and story about the hospice the Point Loma students had set up. The headline read: THE HOUSE THAT GOD BUILT.

Love and marriage. As a pastor, I presided over many weddings, but whenever I got ready to declare that the man and woman were now husband and wife, I stumbled over the need to announce that I was doing so "by the power and authority vested in me by the Commonwealth of Pennsylvania."

I think it would be best to separate church and state and get churches out of the marriage business, at least as it is currently set up. Instead of being legally married at church, couples should be married at the courthouse, and then those Christian couples who choose to do so should be able to celebrate their marriage with a service at their church with family and friends. Surprisingly, a few churches have adopted my proposal. If more broadly embraced, this approach might have avoided decades of culture wars over same-sex marriage.

For the longest time, I approved civil unions for same-sex couples, before I eventually came around to supporting same-sex marriage. Why do I support this? It's simple. Of all the blessings that have nurtured my spiritual life, none has been more important than my marriage to Peggy. Why shouldn't I want my gay and lesbian brothers and sisters to experience this kind of love and spiritual nourishment in their lives?

Many evangelicals seem fixated on seeing homosexual relationships only as sexual, but all meaningful intimate relationships are also spiritual. Marriage was created by God to be mutually edifying. Supporting same-sex marriage seems like the pro-family thing to do.

"*Peggy, you were right!*" Peggy is loving and compassionate, and she has always been more sensitive to people's pain and hurt than I am. She has an acute sensitivity to the pain inflicted on gay people by Christians, and for decades she has counseled AIDS patients and victims of anti-gay hatred, marched in gay pride parades, and demonstrated on behalf of gay rights in DC and outside a Methodist meeting in Cleveland.

For years, people knew that Peggy approved of same-sex marriage and I (then) did not. For years, she and I spoke together on the topic at churches that were struggling to address the issue. As one pastor put it when he invited us: "You two can disagree about this issue but still get along and stay married. Perhaps you can teach our church how to do the same thing."

That pastor did not know that our differences on this issue were a source of tension in our marriage. But over time, hearing Peggy talk during those church dialogues moved me closer to her point of view. In addition, I came to know more devoted Christians who were gay, not through choice but through orientation. I also read my Bible and prayed on the subject.

For the longest time, I believed that God did not bless such unions as he blesses heterosexual unions, but in recent years I have come over to Peggy's side in this debate. After seeing men and women who love Jesus torture themselves over their sexuality, I now believe that God wants all his children—including his gay children—to enjoy the love that can only be found in covenantal marriage.

Not for the first or last time in our marriage, I came to realize that I had been wrong, and Peggy was right. I am grateful that my wife approached our differences on this important issue with love, persistence, and patience. She helped to open my eyes, my mind, and my heart by doing nothing more—and nothing less—than holding me accountable to the core Christian values I hold most dear.

Once again, what had initially seemed to be an intractable religious conflict in my life was resolved by means of a new insight. As always, it was the example and guidance of someone I admire and respect that led to this further evolution of my theology.

Flexing with Fear and Trembling

I'm still trying to work out my salvation and still trying to fine-tune my theology about some of the most challenging issues we face. I am not surprised or disappointed that my views on some issues have changed; in fact, I would be surprised and disappointed if that were not the case. A Christian theology that fails to adapt to new challenges is as worthless as a theology cut off from biblical tradition and nearly two thousand years of church tradition.

I spent many years of my life studying, teaching, and analyzing many subjects from multiple angles. But were my ideas contributing to making the world a better place in concrete ways that change people's lives? Tackling that puzzle would be another step of my spiritual journey.

CHAPTER 17

LET'S DO IT!

People talk about changing the world, but how do you actually do it? The world is big and complicated. How can we make a significant difference? In the 1960s and 1970s, some young people sought to change things by taking part in protests, picketing, marches, and demonstrations such as the peace vigil we held at Penn. More radical young people sought change through revolution, campus occupations, and even bombings.

As I discovered in my studies and teaching, Marxist groups had a clear idea of what the world is and how to change it using Marxist theories. They called this process praxis, which refers to the steps used to put a theory or belief into action. *Praxis* also refers to the ways people change when they become practical about taking their beliefs and values to institutions.

Plato taught that what we think influences what we do. Marx answered by saying that what we do influences what we think and feel. Both are true. Praxis is dialectical: what we think influences what we do, and what we do influences what we think.

Marxists have an ideology and a goal: putting Karl Marx's ideas into effect in governments around the world. Philosophers and theologians also talk about praxis, arguing that great ideas and beliefs are not effective unless they are applied and put into action.

Praxis is important for Christians too. When Jesus talked about love, he was not talking about warm feelings or kind thoughts but about action: "Love your neighbor as yourself" (Matt. 22:39).

James spelled this out in his epistle: "What good is it, my brothers and sisters, if someone claims to have faith but has no deeds? . . . Faith by itself, if it is not accompanied by action, is dead" (James 2:14, 17). Belief itself is not enough: "You believe that there is one God. Good! Even the demons believe that—and shudder" (James 2:19).

When I looked at Christians and how they put their faith into action to improve the world, it seemed their strategy focused primarily on evangelism or missions. The idea was to change individuals through preaching, conversion, and discipleship so that these changed individuals would then change the world. But was that the best approach?

After spending years studying theology in an effort to understand doctrine correctly, I was now trying to figure out how to apply that doctrine to the problems of the world.

Developing a Strategy for Social Change

Students at Eastern continued to work at the Boys Club in Trenton, New Jersey. This was a win-win scenario: the Eastern students were helping needy young people in Trenton, while those needy kids were also helping Eastern students grow in their knowledge and experience about how to help others in practical ways. I was excited about this work, but I felt something more needed to be done, even though I could not figure out exactly what was needed.

My upbringing taught me that if I really wanted to be a good Christian, I had to be a missionary. Although the mission bug continued to eat away at me, I still was not sure that sharing the gospel was the limit of Christians' responsibilities to the world.

I eventually settled on this dual approach:

- We evangelize and disciple people so that they can experience a personal relationship with Jesus and become kingdom people.
- Then we turn these kingdom people loose so they can transform all the institutions of this world into what God wants them to be.

The Campolo Center for Ministry

Evangelism is one way to help the church grow. Another way is to help church leaders become better and more effective leaders. That's the goal of the Campolo Center for Ministry, which was launched at Eastern to "prepare students for servant-leadership in the Church, Christian ministries, and the public sphere—for the glory of God."

Every year at Eastern, and at other colleges throughout the land, corporate recruiters show up on campus during certain weeks of the school year, seeking to hire "the best of the best" graduates for their companies. I think churches should do the same thing by identifying young people in their congregations who are committed to God, who have the capacity for effective communication, and who have a heart for ministry.

My church did not do that, but my mother prompted me to do everything I could do to prepare myself for God's service. This kind of parental guidance has been a long tradition in America. For example, Puritan parents would often choose, dedicate, and train one child in the family to become a minister.

The Campolo Center for Ministry was created to encourage Christian leaders to be the best of the best at what they do. The center seeks candidates who are spiritually gifted, communally called, and vocationally committed to holistic Christian ministry.

Campolo Scholars are expected to pursue God, contribute to the local church, be a good citizen of the Eastern University community, and actively participate in the Campolo Center for Ministry. The center has been privileged to work with and send out many effective and committed Christian servants.

Balancing Spiritual and Practical Ministry

Another realization has emerged from my continuing study of church history. In areas of the world where people suffer economically, robust church growth and the spread of Christian influence on a culture have often flowed from a two-stage strategy that balances spiritual and physical needs:

- *Stage 1*. Missionaries and ministers bring people to Jesus and start churches that will nurture their faith.
- *Stage 2*. Teachers, doctors, agriculturalists, and other skilled servants provide needed practical services to the surrounding community, supporting those churches and giving greater social legitimacy to the church's message.

I knew churches all over the world that were involved in Stage 1 activities to change individuals spiritually, but I did not see as many believers involved in Stage 2 activities that transform communities. Recognizing this gap, I saw a new need and a new opportunity.

But how to go about it? As I sought to follow the advice of Jesus, who compared the kingdom of God to a tiny mustard seed (Matt. 13:31–32), I realized that small things can have mighty effects. With that image in mind, I came to be very involved in microeconomic development for small businesses and cottage industries that needy people could build, own, and run for themselves.

As a social scientist, I also understood that communities can create extended chains of good consequences through seemingly unrelated activities that are actually the result of positive interdependence. For example, in one small-business undertaking, the women in a small village in Haiti bought solar panels and sold the power they harnessed to charge people's cell phones. These women then took their profits and invested them in a bakery that sold loaves of bread in nearby villages. Next, they used their bakery profits to buy a big-screen TV and set up a small theater that charged people a small amount to watch TV shows. So, for this village, new sources of electrical power, food, and community entertainment were all derived, directly or indirectly, from one initial small investment. I am a firm believer in the value of funding microeconomic development projects, which I know are capable of transforming the lives of poor people around the world.

A God Thing

I believe education plays a central role in changing both people and societies. I dreamed of having an opportunity to create a new Christian college somewhere in the developing world. But I was certain I would never have that chance, so I did not share the idea with others.

Never say never, because God works in mysterious ways. During my first year of teaching at Eastern, I was approached by a student who had been to the Dominican Republic on a mission trip with the Christian Medical Society. She told me about meeting a young Dominican doctor there who wanted to start a university in his country. I knew this was one of those "God things," those moments when I could sense the Creator of the cosmos pulling strings to give me the desires of my heart.

Soon, I was on a plane to meet the doctor. We brainstormed together about the idea of a new university. Before we knew it, the president of the Dominican Republic let us know that not only did he wholeheartedly support our effort but he would give us a campus to make it happen. This was just the beginning of my Dominican adventures:

- Eastern University in San Pedro de Macoris opened in 1970. Now known as East Central University, the school operates a medical center in the capital city of Santo Domingo, which is an hour away.
- A sister campus, the Technological University of the South, in Azua, opened a few years later.
- These schools have been successful, changing the lives of students, who then change the culture of their country. But neither of these schools was thoroughly Christian, so we also helped found a third school, the National Evangelical University in Santiago.
- We also worked with Dominican people through a self-help program that paid them for crafts they produced.

All of these were "God things," but they all required earthly money and organization to make them work. The practical needs and requirements of these and other projects were the original impetus for the nonprofit organization we called EAPE.

Organization Man

The Evangelical Association for the Promotion of Education (EAPE) officially came into existence as an independent nonprofit in 1971, but it had actually started a couple of years earlier as an unofficial umbrella organization for the work we were doing in Philadelphia, the Dominican Republic, Haiti, and other locations around the world.

Peggy was the organization's first secretary. Our official mission was "to establish educational institutions in undeveloped countries and to sustain their operation by raising funds and recruiting teachers." I never really liked the organization's long name, which was cooked up by the attorney who drafted our incorporation papers and was always hard to say. We came to refer to it by its initials: EAPE.

C. Everett Koop was a crucial help in our early years. Koop ran an organization called the Light of Life, which supported the start-up and development of new nonprofits. Before we established EAPE, the donations we received for our work went through Light of Life.

People came to me with needs, and I mentioned these needs to some of the students I interacted with at Penn and Eastern. But as some of these projects grew, they needed governance, management, a board of directors, a finance director, and an office to keep all the wheels spinning.

I was EAPE's chief fundraiser, and I turned to the audiences at my growing number of speaking engagements, asking them to contribute to the latest project we were trying to fund. For example, I was asked to lead an evangelism weekend for First Baptist Church of Crawfordsville, Indiana. When I spoke about our work in the Dominican Republic, the pastor pleaded with his congregation to help us. I left there with a check to EAPE for $10,000. The more I spoke, the more I could raise, and the more work we could fund.

I loved the ministry we were doing, which was helping both individuals and communities. As EAPE grew, however, I must admit that I had difficulties with my growing administrative burdens. It's one thing to be the kind of ministry entrepreneur who launches projects, but it's a completely different skill set to keep these projects operating as they should. Unfortunately for me, and for those who chose to work with me, my abilities in the former did not translate into skill in the latter. The tensions between these conflicting duties would torture me for many years.

Change Agent

I had a dream of changing a developing country through education, and the work EAPE did in the Dominican Republic more than fulfilled this dream. Meanwhile, another change was taking place closer to home.

As more Eastern students became more involved in the ministry projects of EAPE, the school took steps to connect this work to the academic curriculum. In the early 1970s, Eastern developed an undergraduate program in social work, becoming only the second college in the United States to create an accredited social-work program.

EAPE also played a critical role in creating a master's program in microeconomic development, a program that reflected my two-stage view of social change. When I saw the economic effects of the small cottage industries we established in the Dominican Republic and Haiti, I knew missions would need to be connected to economic development.

Poor countries need doctors, teachers, agronomists, and agriculturalists who can help people thrive in all areas of life. But instead of importing these leaders from elsewhere, countries need to find indigenous leaders in their midst. Local churches assist in this effort by nurturing people and helping them become leaders who can build businesses and cottage industries that they own and run themselves and that employ local people. We cannot ignore the important link between missions and economic development.

The training in microeconomic development offered by Eastern's MBA program has enabled many people to start small businesses that create jobs for people who need them, both in American inner cities and around the world. Since its founding, this one MBA program has helped create 150,000 jobs that lifted people out of poverty.

Accept Christ and His Cross

We closed EAPE in 2014, after more than forty years of transformative ministry around the world. It was a good run. I am proud of the positive differences that EAPE was able to make, thanks to the many people who served, donated, and helped run the organization. I was thrilled to be part of God's big plan to help people grow spiritually, economically, socially, and in every other way. When I preached or spoke in churches, I tried to offer people two challenges: accept Christ's loving salvation and take up his cross in grateful service. You cannot separate the two, I emphasized.

When we closed EAPE, about $100,000 in assets remained, after all of the organization's financial obligations had been settled. Our board decided to give these funds to Eastern University to provide seed money to start the Campolo Center for Ministry. I was honored and pleased by that decision, and I felt that it was consistent with the aims of EAPE. The Campolo Center provides scholarships and support to committed Christian students who want to grow in their faith and be used by God in the world. This program has helped support many worthy students who sought to minister to the world. In many ways, I see it as an important part of the legacy of EAPE.

PART 4

PUBLIC THEOLOGIAN

CHAPTER 18

CAMPOLO FOR CONGRESS '76

In my life, 1976 was a wonderful, glorious year. Americans were feeling patriotic as they celebrated the nation's bicentennial year. Jimmy Carter, a born-again Christian who was the Democrats' candidate for president, was one of three Christians running, which led *Newsweek* to call it "The Year of the Evangelicals."

I joined the patriotic fervor, announcing my candidacy to represent Pennsylvania's Fifth Congressional District in the United States Congress. After my many years behind church pulpits and college podiums, I wanted to serve in a new way. This would be the year to take my theology to political meetings and coffee gatherings hosted in the homes of my supporters.

Once again, I was entering a new environment and being introduced to new people and ideas. I became friends with many local political operatives, most of whom had no Christian or religious affiliations. Years after my campaign, these friends called me to officiate at their weddings and family funerals because I was the only clergy person they knew.

At the time, I was reading widely on the subject of principalities and powers, which Paul described in Ephesians 6:12: "For our struggle is not against flesh and blood, but against the rulers, against the authorities, against the powers of this dark world and against the spiritual forces of evil in the heavenly realms."

As a sociologist, I understood Paul to be addressing the social institutions and forces that we humans create. Then, in turn, these institutions create and shape us in their image. I believed that government was one of the principalities and powers that needed to be under the lordship of Christ, and I wanted to do my part.

Like President Carter, I was a Democrat. Back then, evangelical Christians still voted for Democrats. That would change in 1980, after the religious right supported Ronald Reagan for president. The marriage of Christian conservatives and the Republican Party now leads many evangelicals to condemn Democrats as anti-American or demonic. Times have certainly changed.

I was opposed to the huge sums of money that special-interest groups used to buy influence in Congress. Like humorist Will Rogers, I believed that "we have the best Congress money can buy." So, I made a radical decision. I pledged to take no more than $50 from any one donor. Some called my principled decision impractical because I raised only $18,000 for my campaign, while my Republican opponent raised and spent hundreds of thousands of dollars.

My campaign would be a family affair. Our campaign office was the sunporch of our home on Glenmary Lane in St. Davids. Peggy was my press secretary, and she used creative means to attract good coverage in local papers. Lisa went from door to door, asking residents in various neighborhoods to vote for her dad. Bart took campaign literature to train stations early in the morning to catch commuters. We went outside of the family for one important position: my campaign chairman was a local Catholic priest.

In the end, it was not enough. I received only 43 percent of the vote. But although that showing was a decisive loss, it was also a dramatic improvement over the 18 percent that the previous Democratic candidate had attracted two years earlier.

The voters decided not to send me to Washington, but my adventure in politics taught me much about the political process and deepened my love for American democracy.

The Politics of Milk

My political odyssey had actually begun decades earlier, while I was serving as a pastor in New Jersey. A group of local dairy farmers, some of them members of my church, asked if I could help them do something about the government-mandated prices for their milk, which were ridiculously low.

I knew nothing about the politics of commodity prices, but I was their pastor and wanted to help, so I studied the issue. Some of the milk farmers wanted to start a union that could represent their interests, but they were legally prohibited from this action by the Taft-Hartley Act of 1947.

In desperation, some farmers poured milk down drains to protest the low prices they were being paid. In response, companies began importing more milk from Canada and Scandinavian countries, hurting the US farmers even more.

The protests also backfired with consumers. News photos of farmers dumping milk down drains angered people concerned about world hunger. Discouraged and desperate, the farmers turned to me.

"You've been in the news and on TV," they said. "Can you help us make our case to the public?"

Thanks to my students at Penn, I knew how to organize protests and marches, so that's what I proposed to the farmers. We would gather in Bordentown, march about seven miles to the New Jersey State House in Trenton, and hold a rally to make our case for higher prices.

Initially, some of the farmers were reluctant to march because that's what hippies and angry people did. But I reminded the farmers that protesting and making a case to the public were hallmarks of American democracy, and most agreed.

We planned and proceeded with our march, and we attracted quite a large crowd. Most of the farmers marched together in their overalls. A couple of farmers drove their tractors. One even drove his tractor down the street pulling a flatbed truck that carried a milk cow. I wonder what she thought of the proceedings.

As we made our way to the state capitol, we sang a song I had written for the occasion. My father was a union supporter, and I had learned classic labor songs like "Which Side Are You On?" and "Solidarity Forever." In my studies of labor movements, I saw how songs, some based on popular hymns, brought people together behind the labor movement.

I based my song on the hymn "Must Jesus Bear This Cross Alone?" These are the original words:

> Must Jesus bear this cross alone
> And all the world go free?
> No, there's a cross for everyone
> And there's a cross for me.

My revised version offered these lines—admittedly less inspirational, but still sung with great gusto:

> Must the farmer bear the cost alone
> And all of us go free?
> So there'll be milk for all of us,
> And a glass for you and me.

When we arrived at the capitol, we started setting up our sound system across the street, but a group of state troopers tried to prevent us from holding our rally there. They did not realize I was a veteran preacher, so I did not need any sound system.

"They wouldn't stop Martin Luther King Jr. from meeting here across from the people's capitol," I called out. "They wouldn't keep Jesse Jackson or the NAACP from protesting here. But they try to stop our hardworking dairy farmers who are trying to get decent pay for their milk!"

Dad would have been proud.

Our big march caused a huge traffic jam in downtown Trenton

that day, which was exactly what we wanted. Farmers and milk were front-page news in the region's newspapers the next morning.

It worked. Politicians in New Jersey heard us and said they would help us change the base price for milk. Who wants to be seen as anti-milk? Within a week they had taken action, arranging for a congressional hearing. Congress heard and quickly addressed our concerns. Soon milk's base price was raised substantially. God bless America!

Overnight, a preacher and professor who had never milked a cow in his life became a hometown political hero to a bunch of hardworking farmers. I was amazed by what we had accomplished by organizing, taking action, and rallying the public around a worthy cause. Unfortunately, I was unable, years later, to parlay this early political victory in the milk price wars into a successful campaign for a seat in Congress.

Two Kingdoms

I ran for public office in the hope of making America a little more like God's kingdom. Seizing on the celebration of patriotism inspired by the bicentennial, I appealed to voters: "We need to apply the values of 1776 to the challenges we face in 1976. It's time for a new beginning of American democracy!"

My campaign slogan captured my focus: "We can't fight the war on poverty here and the war in Vietnam at the same time."

I was laser-focused on two issues I thought were connected: poverty and the war in Vietnam. I opposed the United States military's support for B-1 bombers, which cost $150 million each and were criticized as poorly performing white elephants.

I had the support of young people, three hundred of whom joined me in the march that launched my campaign. But other voters questioned me: "Isn't caring for the poor the responsibility of the church, and not the government?"

"Yes, Christians must care for the poor, just as Jesus commanded us," I replied. "But not all Christians do that. And realistically, the church isn't capable of providing all the benefits provided through welfare, government food programs, help to children with disabilities, and other social programs."

I was a two-issue candidate with no real public-policy background or practical agenda, as my Republican competitor Richard T. Schulze made all too clear to the voters. Schulze, who refused to debate me during the campaign, was shrewd in taking what I had considered to be my strengths and revealing them as shortcomings. He argued that people should vote for me only if they wanted to send a philosopher or theologian to Congress. For those with real-world problems, who needed help in cutting through government bureaucracy that might be holding up a driver's license or Social Security checks, for example, Schulze was the man for the job.

He was right, and the voters decided that the United States could enter its third century just fine without my political leadership. Schulze was elected in 1976 and reelected in the next eight congressional elections.

After the dust settled, Schulze and I had lunch together. That would be unusual today, but back then, politics was not yet fully poisoned by the acrimony we see today. Later on, when Schulze's daughter wanted to attend a Christian college to study sociology, she came to Eastern and studied with me, and she later became a social worker.

I was disappointed there would be no Representative Campolo in Congress, and every two years after that 1976 election, I would briefly consider giving it another try before coming to my senses. Still, my ill-fated campaign had a major effect on my future, as it marked a year of decisions and a shift toward a far more public-facing speaking career than I could ever have imagined.

Decision Time

While I had been gearing up for my congressional campaign, I faced another crucial decision. I was teaching full-time at both

Eastern and Penn while also running for Congress and speaking around the country. It was too much, as the dean of the sociology department at Penn told me one day late in 1975. I had to figure out what I would do and what I would leave behind.

I agonized over my decision between Eastern and Penn. I was inclined to choose Penn, believing that the Ivy League school would be better for my academic résumé, my public speaking, and our family income. Only divine intervention would change my course.

I was sitting at my desk in my office at Penn, gathering the final few materials I would take to the faculty meeting to make my case to stay at the school, when something unexpected happened. God spoke directly to me with great clarity. It was one of the few times in my life that that has ever happened. His message to me was clear: I should leave Penn and stay at Eastern.

I called Peggy right away, telling her about my divine encounter and my sense that God was calling me to make Eastern my home. I remember expressing my concerns about money and how staying at Eastern would mean we would need to live on less.

Her response was classic Peggy: "Tony, if this is what God is telling you to do, then do it. We'll get along, no matter what. We always have." I walked down the hall to the faculty meeting with mixed feelings but clarity of purpose. When I got there, I let them know I was withdrawing my name for consideration for the faculty position.

It was one of the best decisions God ever made for me. From then on, Eastern would be the permanent base of operations for all of my speaking, writing, and organizing work.

CHAPTER 19

ON THE ROAD AGAIN

When I answered the phone, it was George Verwer, the leader of a ministry called Operation Mobilization (OM), on the line. It was the early 1970s, and George said he wanted me to fly to San Diego to speak for a fundraiser at a local church. Operation Mobilization had recently lost one of the ships that served as its sailing medical hospitals, bringing treatment and healing to poor people around the world, among other functions. George said the ministry needed a new ship, and he wanted me to help raise the funds.

"You want me to fly all the way out there to speak?" I asked George, shocked and confused by his offer. "You want me to travel almost three thousand miles to give a single talk?"

George was insistent, so I booked the flight, but I remained dubious that I could fulfill the mission. When I reached the church, I was even more underwhelmed. It was a small church, and we were meeting in a dingy basement. The evening started with dinner, and looking at the small group of people there, I thought they were not wealthy enough to generate the kind of donations George was seeking. But I put my heart into the talk, letting the audience know how Operation Mobilization was spreading the gospel throughout Africa, something it did with great success.

"Well, I hope I helped OM raise a few bucks," I told George

the next morning, before I flew back home. I was doubtful that my talk to the small audience had done much good.

"You did great, Tony," George said. "One man who attended the dinner is going to give us half a million dollars, and other donors gave a combined half a million too. We're going to be able to buy a new ship. I'm so grateful to you, and so thankful to God." You could have knocked me over with a feather.

I had spent years preaching from church pulpits and teaching in college classrooms. And during my congressional campaign, I added political stump speeches. I also spoke at churches and colleges around the Northeast. But during the seventies and eighties, my range expanded. I traveled more widely and more often for speaking engagements, and I became a popular speaker not only at churches but also at parachurch events, youth-worker conventions, and even secular corporate gatherings. I would fly into a town; be picked up and whisked off to an event where I might speak to hundreds or thousands of people, and occasionally even tens of thousands of people; and then be taken back to the airport so I could fly home again. For a long while, I had between three hundred and five hundred speaking engagements a year. It was a hectic pace.

My expanded career as a speaker inflated my ego. People were paying me more and more money to speak to larger and larger groups. At large festivals, I might share a message with thirty thousand or forty thousand young people at once. I began to think of myself as a big shot, and I am glad Peggy reminded me of my real status.

"A big shot is really nothing more than a little shot, except he's five hundred miles away from home," she told me.

Friday, Sunday, and Beyond

Over the years, the powerful refrain of the Reverend Doctor Dennie W. Hoggard's "It's Friday, but Sunday's Comin'" sermon had always stayed with me. Pastor Hoggard was the longtime pastor of Mt. Carmel Baptist Church, which is where I had heard him deliver it, at a Good Friday service long ago. Pastor Hoggard's sermon described how Jesus's disciples must have felt about their Savior's death on Good Friday, when they were still unaware that he would miraculously rise from the dead on Sunday. It's a great message for people who are feeling down, discouraged, and in need of encouragement and inspiration.

In other words, it's a message that lots of people really need to hear.

Pastor Hoggard was a master preacher, and I remember an observation he shared with me about the different preaching styles he'd seen. "White preachers tend to get excited and raise their voices when they're angry about something," he told me. "We Black preachers raise our voices and shout when we're happy about something."

I tried to focus on the happy parts of that sermon when, near the close of my congressional run, I wanted to give a little inspiration to the party officials and volunteers who were supporting my campaign. I had been given no chance of beating a popular Republican incumbent. So, with the odds of winning stacked against me, I wanted to share a message of hope and faith, and "Sunday's Comin'" fit the bill perfectly. It also gave me a chance to share my faith with people who supported me and did not seem to have a relationship with Christ. I explained how the power of Christ's resurrection can transform lives and change our world.

My 1976 channeling of "It's Friday, but Sunday's Comin'" for the local Democratic party leaders and campaign volunteers went over very well. Soon I was revising the talk to preach it at a few nearby churches and student groups. People began to share cassette tapes of my talk with one another, and over time it became my signature talk.

I borrowed just about the whole sermon, and I did my best to channel Pastor Hoggard in my delivery. The generous Pastor

Hoggard was fine with that, for which I will always be grateful. I made a few tweaks here and there, and I used a framing device to set it up and make it my own. Eventually, I would share this theme so many times, in so many places, and with so many people, that if it were not so well-designed and durable, I surely would have worn it out.

A cassette tape of my version of this talk wound up in the hands of James Dobson, the founder of Focus on the Family. He loved my talk and asked me if he could share it on his daily radio broadcast, which was one of the most popular Christian programs. I said yes, and Focus played my talk every Easter weekend for a number of years and sold tens of thousands of copies of the tape, with all proceeds supporting Focus.

Challenging Youth Workers

Another important phone call came to me during the 1970s, this time from an organization called Youth Specialties. Its leaders had heard my talk and wanted me to present it to a large audience at its annual convention in Atlanta.

Youth ministry is one of the most challenging, most rewarding, and poorest-paying jobs in churches. I was thrilled to speak to these young leaders, who had a deep interest in social and theological issues I had explored with my students at Eastern and Penn.

Youth workers are generally tuned in to the cultural differences that influence the different ways in which young people and adults approach Christianity. Often, young people are attracted to Jesus and are more radical in their faith, while their parents have gradually embraced a more culturally conditioned faith. I could speak to youth workers about racism and Christian nationalism, things I would have difficulty discussing with their parents.

"God created us in his image, and we decided to return the favor by creating him in our image!" I would say, using a remark

I had borrowed from George Bernard Shaw. That would always draw a big laugh from the crowd, but youth workers understood that this funny line conveyed a profound truth. When we work with young people, we want to bring them to faith in Jesus, not faith in our culture's warped image of Jesus.

My experience teaching sociology helped me create a style of speaking that seemed to go over well with young Christian audiences. At a time when older people complained about the generation gap, young people seemed to understand me perfectly when I talked about how many American Christians had replaced a biblical Jesus with a cultural Jesus who incarnates American values, which is idolatry.

"If you follow Jesus's radical teachings, you will be somebody who does not affirm American values as much as he critiques those American values," I told them.

Another of my stock lines was well-received by youth workers: "If you visit Las Vegas or New York City, you might conclude that God owes Sodom and Gomorrah an apology."

Success was an important topic because youth workers were under significant pressure to be successful. Even if they served a small church, they were expected to attract a large youth group and to persuade all the kids in the youth group to be dedicated Christians. The youth workers applauded when I shared Mother Teresa's remark that "Christ calls you to be faithful rather than successful." They loved that.

My goal was to encourage undivided devotion to the real Jesus, not to tear down America. But some patriotic Christians were offended when I suggested that America was something less than a perfectly Christian country.

"Christianity was born in Israel as a religion," I would say in another borrowed line. "Then they took it to Rome and made it into an organization. They took it to Europe and made it into a culture. Then they took it to America, and we made it into a business enterprise."

I would speak at dozens of youth-worker gatherings in the coming decades, challenging these leaders to follow Christ as committed disciples and to wholeheartedly encourage the church's next generation to do the same. Youth Specialties gave me a Lifetime Achievement Award, which said that I "defined and courageously pioneered what it means to encourage, care, and lead students." To this day, that recognition remains very special to me.

My Brief Film Career

Eventually, a cassette tape of "Sunday's Comin'" wound up in the hands of executives at Word Publishing, who wanted me to do a film that could be shown to youth groups and Sunday-school classes, and later a book. I flew to Texas to film the talk before an enthusiastic group of Baylor University students.

I showed up for the filming in my usual old, worn, corduroy jacket. Joey Paul, the executive in charge of the filming, was aghast. He felt that my attire screamed "underpaid college professor." He quickly took me to a men's clothing store, where we bought a couple of nice blazers and pairs of trousers, to make me more presentable for the cameras. I wore those clothes for years and years after the filming, and Joey's wardrobe choices for me became the permanent foundation of my work uniform.

Churches used this movie in Sunday-school classes and youth groups for many years. After the success of the film, we created a four-part film series called *You Can Make a Difference*. This was then turned into a book, which won a Gold Medallion Book Award from the Evangelical Publishers Association.

I loved doing these projects, which were filmed live in front of enthusiastic young audiences. And I loved getting paid for doing those films, which enabled Peggy and me to finally buy our first family house, where we would live for the next quarter century.

Adapting the Message

Some speakers have a popular speech that they give time and time again with minimal changes. I stuck with a few stock speeches and regularly revised them, inserting new information that came from current events or recent academic research. And when I was asked to speak at youth gatherings, I always asked the people in charge what they hoped to accomplish, and I tried to fulfill their objectives, adapting each talk to their specific audience and needs.

My different talks employed different rhetorical styles.

When I spoke on college campuses, I wanted to make sure I honored academic and intellectual callings, which are too often demeaned by some anti-intellectual evangelicals. In these talks, I would speak as Professor Campolo, using more citations and references to major secular authors and current sociological research than I used in my church talks.

When I spoke at missions conferences, I tried to be prophetic, calling young people to follow Jesus's call to go and make disciples of all nations. I would speak about my experience overseas with EAPE and stress the importance of serving others when you are young and relatively unencumbered by things like marriage, kids, and mortgage payments.

Still, I was never comfortable when people suggested I was a "prophet," which Christianity Today did in a 2003 cover story calling me "The Positive Prophet." CT editor Ted Olsen captured my conflicted feelings about this label in this quote from me:

> When I think of a prophet, I think of somebody who has a word from God and speaks with authority that comes from that revelation. I wish that when I spoke I had that. . . . I read the Bible, I speak through issues, I see what I think is hypocrisy in the church and things that are wrong, and I speak to these things. But I could be wrong.[3]

Pretty soon, Compassion International began promoting me to speak at colleges and universities, often alongside Christian musicians. Compassion soon discovered that my talk worked just as well without musicians, so it also sent me out alone to speak and recruit young men and women to become child sponsors through Compassion, which is something Peggy and I had done for years.

Because I was effective at stirring audiences and raising donations, I became a speaker for city rescue missions, mission groups like Youth With a Mission, and SonScape Retreats, which offers times of rest and renewal in Colorado for Christian leaders and their spouses. Peggy and I were ourselves helped by a SonScape retreat we attended.

I also started receiving more offers to speak in the United Kingdom. Compassion's affiliate in the United Kingdom sponsored a week-long tour across Scotland with musician Graham Kendrick. Peggy and I loved touring this beautiful country and meeting believers there. I also spoke at an annual event called Spring Harvest (which became known as Greenbelt and grew into one of England's largest Christian gatherings) and at an evangelistic rally in Perth, Scotland, organized by the Billy Graham Evangelistic Association.

When speaking to Christians and trying to raise support for these ministries, I would often adopt a judgmental approach, similar to an Old Testament prophet, urging them to confess and repent of their indifference to the plight of poor and oppressed people around the world. I'm sure some people made donations to ease some of the guilt I tried to inspire.

In many of these talks, I quoted Jesus's words in Matthew 25 about the sheep and the goats and our obligation to care for the people he called "the least of these." My interpretation of Jesus's words would later land me in hot water with some modern-day Inquisitors.

When I spoke at church services and spiritual retreats, I suddenly became Pastor Tony all over again. I enjoyed opportunities to be pastoral and talk to my brothers and sisters about how we can work together to follow Jesus's commands to love God and love one another.

I also spoke in secular business settings, including a number of talks to the sales staff of insurance companies. I typically saw these corporate talks as evangelistic opportunities, including the time I spoke to hundreds of life-insurance underwriters in Kuala Lumpur, Malaysia. Organizers asked for a copy of my notes from my talk, which they distributed to the insurance executives, many of whom were Muslims.

I once talked with the Reverend Robert Schuller about evangelism. He told me that there are some people who like to scare people into heaven, and there are others who just want to hold up Jesus and show him as so appealing that people will want to have a relationship with him. Schuller always followed that second approach, and I did too.

When I spoke to secular audiences, I asked God to help me find ways to communicate who Jesus was and what he was all about without making them angry with me or with God. I tried to say, "I'm a Christian, and this is what Christians believe," instead of saying, "This is what Christians believe, and you're going to hell if you don't believe it too."

Peggy joined me at some of these secular talks, and she smiled to see how far I could go in presenting the gospel to secular audiences while also making sure I inspired them to sell a few more insurance policies.

The Irony of Celebrity

As a preacher and sociology professor, I often talked about the dangers of the cult of celebrity. But suddenly, the sociologist who regularly issued critiques of celebrity culture had himself become something of a celebrity, at least in certain circles. The preacher who routinely railed against the accumulation of worldly wealth was himself growing wealthy. I often donated my speaking fees to EAPE or other ministries, but the Campolos were feeling no pain.

I was not the only person who saw the irony in these circumstances. My son, Bart, who studied at Haverford College, a Quaker school, noted my hypocrisy.

"You're preaching one thing but doing another," he said. "You preach about poverty, but you make a good income from that preaching."

On the other hand, my success on the speaking circuit gave me important opportunities to partner with ministries like Compassion and World Vision, helping them raise millions of dollars and serve thousands of the neediest children in the world.

I grew up in a poor immigrant family that struggled to make ends meet. I guess I still have not adjusted to having enough money to buy what I need or want. I loved the speaking, but I was not sure I loved what it might be doing to change me.

For some reason, people continued to invite me to speak, and I continued to accept as many of those invitations as I could until my stroke halted my globetrotting ways.

I estimate that I spoke to a quarter-million to a half-million people over the years. No matter the setting, I always followed the model of Billy Graham and invited my listeners to accept Christ and/or follow him more closely. I look forward to catching up with some of those folks in my next life.

CHAPTER 20

FREE-RANGE THEOLOGY

I apparently missed the warning in Ecclesiastes 12:12: "Of making many books there is no end, and much study wearies the body." In the course of my career, I have written and collaborated on fifty books. I wrote my first book in 1971. I waited a decade before I wrote my next book. Then, during the 1980s and 1990s, I published thirty-one books.

What was the cause of my expansive literary output? Did I suddenly give up on teaching and preaching to write? No. As my speaking career took off, publishers wanted me to write more books because popular speakers sell books. Editors from Word, Thomas Nelson, Zondervan, InterVarsity Press, Regal, and others repeatedly asked me to do books based on my talks and sell the published books at my speaking engagements. That approach worked so well with my book *It's Friday, but Sunday's Comin'* that we followed that model with other books.

It seemed that Christians were wrestling with a number of theological and cultural questions that needed answers. I have always felt that when someone asks a legitimate question, they deserve a legitimate answer. When people asked me questions in my classes or my public talks, I tried to respond with answers based on the Bible, Christian theology, and everything I was studying as a sociologist. I have always believed that theology is a discipline that comes up with answers to the complex questions people ask. Now, I was being given the opportunity to come up with Christ-centered answers to the many questions people were asking about faith, morality, social issues, and politics.

As a pastor, I preached from the Bible, teaching believers how to live as faithful disciples of Christ. As a professor, I taught students to use the tools of sociology to read their world. Now, in my new calling as a public speaker and author, I was a free-range theologian, addressing a host of spiritual and cultural issues audiences were concerned about.

I did not have the luxury of using a writer's retreat or hideaway so I could focus my mind, turn out the world's distractions, and write to my heart's content. I was still teaching full-time, and my speaking and preaching schedule was increasingly full. So, I wrote my books in longhand on legal notepads, in bits and pieces, from planes, trains, and hotels. Then I would turn everything over to Peggy, who would type everything, cleaning up most of my many mistakes. Then we would send the manuscript off to a publisher and get to work on the next project.

It was crazy, but it was exciting and gratifying, too, because it gave me the opportunity to apply my faith to some of the thorniest issues of the day and to help fellow believers do the same. Here's a sampling of some of the topics I tackled.

What Does It Mean to Be Successful in America?

Two of my earliest books tackled myths of success and power that are woven into our understanding of the American dream. *The Success Fantasy* (1980) looked at how so many people use false standards to assess how successful they are, leading to feelings of emptiness and emotional bankruptcy that can only be transformed by a reliance on God's unchanging standards.

The Power Delusion (1983) dealt with "power trips" (when a boss or political leader relishes exercising control over underlings) and taught that a Christian should be more focused on love than power.

Wealth

Wealth often follows professional success, and as I often told my audiences, "There's nothing wrong with making a million dollars as long as you don't selfishly keep it, but use it as Jesus would have used it."

One of my books was 1988's *20 Hot Potatoes Christians Are Afraid to Touch*, which explored twenty different topics, including AIDS, homosexuality, women preachers, public schools, psychological counseling, and working mothers.

One of the chapters in *Hot Potatoes* was "Can Wealthy People Get into Heaven (or, Can a Christian Own a BMW?)" The chapter was inspired by questions I received from young people who wondered why so many churches seemed to favor wealthy people, even though Jesus warned, "Truly I tell you, it is hard for someone who is rich to enter the kingdom of heaven. Again I tell you, it is easier for a camel to go through the eye of a needle than for someone who is rich to enter the kingdom of God" (Matt. 19:23–24).

This chapter came from my speaking. I raised the BMW question when I spoke at Urbana '87, the missionary conference sponsored by InterVarsity Christian Fellowship. I cited the work of Thorstein Veblen, a sociologist who coined the phrase "conspicuous consumption" to describe the spending we do to impress our neighbors.

Does a Cadillac ride so much better than a Chevy that it's worth the many additional thousands of dollars? Not really. We buy the Cadillac as a signifier, to show others how successful we are.

I thought that BMWs and other costly cars were clear symbols of conspicuous consumption, but my beef was not about cars. I turned the BMW into a metaphor, asking, "What's your BMW?" I argued that an expensive Brooks Brothers suit could be someone's BMW.

The point was not to harass people about their luxury goods, but to reaffirm Anabaptist theology on worldly wealth: "Christians are called to live simply so that others can simply live."

That chapter generated calls and letters from people who were upset with me and felt I was condemning BMWs and capitalism. One letter I received, from a man in Texas, enclosed a BMW key and let me know that he had paid a local auto dealer for a new BMW, for me. All I needed to do was come to Texas and pick it up. His letter ended with a postscript: "Don't make any more snide remarks about BMWs, because you're one of us now."

I wrote the man back and informed him that as soon as I got the car I would sell it and send the funds to EAPE, our mission organization. Realizing that I would not be budged, he wrote back, enclosing a check in the amount of the BMW's price.

The Environment

The first Earth Day was celebrated in 1970, and concern about the environment only grew after that. Many evangelicals initially joined in, promoting "Creation care" and "environmental stewardship" through the '70s and '80s. But that changed in the '90s as white evangelicals married their movement to the GOP and its "Drill, baby, drill" ethos. Today, evangelicals largely deny climate change and label Christian environmentalists as nature-worshipping pagans. Although it was Republican president Richard Nixon who created the Environmental Protection Agency, many evangelicals knew that New Age adherents supported environmentalism and concluded that therefore it must not be a Christian issue.

Today, many deeply conservative ministries teach that environmentalism is a pagan religious movement and that Christians who promote "creation care" are trying to import this pagan heresy into the Christian faith. They seem to believe that the one thing worse than environmental pollution is environmental protection.

I came to the opposite conclusion in two books I published in 1992: *How to Rescue the Earth without Worshiping Nature: A Christian's Call to Save Creation* and *50 Ways You Can Save the Planet*.

"Being concerned about the environment is a biblically mandated command, and acting to rescue creation is a Christian obligation," I wrote. "Each of us has a responsibility to do something about our polluted and trashed creation right now. In anticipation of his [Jesus's] coming, we must go to work today and contribute to the work which he will complete on the day of his coming."

I find it ironic that evangelical conservations are often skeptical of the environmental conservation movement. After all, what could be more conservative than conservation?

I concur with Francis Schaeffer's 1970 book, *Pollution and the Death of Man*. Schaeffer said that even though God wanted humans to be faithful stewards who lovingly cared for his creation, secular thinkers and citizens have played a bigger role in creation care than Christians have. Believers should have been at the forefront of this movement, but it was secular groups, not the church, that sensitized people to human-caused environmental degradation and climate change.

Politics and Faith

My 1995 book *Is Jesus a Republican or a Democrat? And 14 Other Polarizing Issues*, addressed the growing politicization of faith by conservative Christian activists. Many Christians have embraced conservative politics, believing it is Christian, but Jesus was a radical whose values transcend partisan politics.

Evangelicals should have learned about the dangers of partisan politics from mainline Protestant denominations that married themselves to liberal politics in the 1960s and 1970s and lost many millions of members. I wrote about this in my 1995 book *Can Mainline Denominations Make a Comeback?*

At the time I was still hopeful that mainline groups, including Presbyterians and Lutherans, would eventually wake up and realize they needed to engage in traditional evangelism and win people to Christ. Without evangelism, I warned, mainline churches would continue to die, and sadly, that's what has happened.

Today, more and more evangelical churches are giving up on evangelism and promoting political activism as the preferred means to change the world. The politics differ: mainliners are liberals, while most evangelicals are on the right.

But the problem for the church is the same: evangelicals are substituting political advocacy for Christ's gospel. And the results are dispiriting. Today, evangelical churches are losing members as more and more people grow tired of hearing partisan political sermons.

Women in the Church and the Home

I grew up in churches full of female Christian-education directors, Sunday-school directors, youth directors, and missionaries. There was just one place these wonderful women could not go: the pulpit. I addressed this issue in my *Hot Potatoes* chapter "What about Women Preachers?"

I wrestled with New Testament passages and church history before concluding that "too often . . . reasons for opposing the ordination of women are hidden by theological rationalizations generated by religious male chauvinists." I argued that at least part of the restriction was based on economics. Many male preachers were simply afraid of the competition.

As I wrote, "Evangelical Christianity has evidenced a hypocritical duplicity by sending women to be preachers in difficult situations overseas while denying them the right to be ministers in the United States."

A recent example of this prejudice was clear in 2023 when the Southern Baptist Convention (SBC) continued to delay work on a promised database of SBC pastors who had sexually abused congregants, but voted quickly to expel Rick Warren's influential Saddleback Community Church for welcoming a woman as a pastor.

My mother deeply influenced my thinking about women preachers. As a girl, she dreamed of becoming one herself, and despite her lack of formal education, she was a gifted speaker and a natural evangelist. She was denied the opportunity to have a real preaching career, solely because she was a woman. What a pity that the church has not always encouraged the preaching gifts of all talented members of the body of Christ to be shared, simply because of gender bias.

Even with the effects of gender bias, however, some women do find their way to the pulpit. Sometimes, this results from a woman's long-standing desire to speak and preach. But sometimes, a woman may find herself in a pulpit or at a podium even if she had no particular desire or ambition to be there. I have seen this happen, more than once, because of a woman's conviction that God has called on her to share an important message.

This was the case with Peggy. Peggy has never relished public speaking or sought the spotlight. So imagine my surprise, and Peggy's, when she felt moved to begin speaking and preaching about God's love for everyone in the LGBTQ community and the need for welcoming and affirming church communities.

By stepping forward and speaking out, despite her natural reluctance to be in the spotlight, she has ministered effectively and brought comfort and peace to many in need. The path of a preacher does not always begin at a seminary.

Are Evangelicals Too Pro-Israel?

I was worried that this *Hot Potatoes* chapter would get me in real trouble. Evangelicals' love for biblical prophecies made many enthusiastic supporters of Israel. But I addressed how the creation of the nation of Israel in 1948 created huge problems for the many Palestinians who were forced from their homelands. These problems are still with us.

"I believe we must urge our Jewish friends to do for others what they would have others do for them," I wrote. Jews also need to "understand the hunger of the Palestinians for a homeland of their own." And I added, "Evangelicals must be pro-Israel but they must also be pro-justice for Arabs."

The condemnation I feared never came. Actually, quite the opposite happened. A group of Christians in Israel invited me to come speak at a unique conference called Christ at the Checkpoint, which explored what Christians should do to address the Palestinian issue. During that event, people repeatedly told me how upset they were that American evangelicals were so pro-Israel that they were actually preventing the Israeli government from addressing the crisis.

Putting Faith into Action

Many of my books are aimed at helping Christians find creative ways to apply their faith to important issues of the day and practical ways to jump-start their outreach. They include the following:

Ideas for Social Action: A Handbook on Mission and Service for Christian Young People
Wake Up America! Answering God's Radical Call while Living in the Real World
50 Ways You Can Feed a Hungry World
50 Ways You Can Share Your Faith

50 Ways You Can Be Pro-Life
50 Ways You Can Reach the World
101 Ways Your Church Can Change the World

I have drawn more heavily on my academic experience as a sociologist in other books, such as these:

The Church and the American Teenager
Sociology through the Eyes of Faith

I have written about spirituality, too, encouraging believers to explore the fruits and gifts of the Holy Spirit in *How to Be Pentecostal without Speaking in Tongues*.

One of my more perceptive critics once said that I have never had an unpublished thought. Perhaps there's some truth in that. All I know is that if I think I have something to say, and especially if I think I have something God wants me to say, I will always find a way to say it.

CHAPTER 21

CAPITALIST CRUSADER

I'm starting this chapter with two statements that may surprise some people, especially my critics: I am a loyal capitalist, and I believe capitalism is the world's best economic system. I have believed these two things for many, many years, but that has not stopped some of my critics from falsely calling me a communist or socialist. The reason is this: even though I embrace capitalism, I have been very critical of capitalism when it works in ways that hurt people, especially the poor.

My battles with capitalism have not been inspired by Marx's *Communist Manifesto*, however. They have been inspired by Jesus, who announced his mission by quoting the prophet Isaiah:

> The Spirit of the Lord is on me,
> because he has anointed me
> to proclaim good news to the poor.
> He has sent me to proclaim freedom for
> the prisoners
> and recovery of sight for the blind,
> to set the oppressed free,
> to proclaim the year of the Lord's favor.
>
> (Luke 4:18–19)

The biblical inspiration for my critique of capitalism is primary. But of course, my thinking about capitalism and Christianity has also been influenced by other sources:

- Karl Marx, for his sociological critiques of capitalism, not his *Communist Manifesto*;
- Walter Rauschenbusch, a Baptist pastor whose 1907 book, *Christianity and the Social Crisis*, was a social-gospel classic;
- The Dutch theologian Hendrik Berkhof, whose book *Christ and the Powers* explored the principalities and powers Paul cited in Ephesians 6:12. Berkhof taught that the principalities and powers that believers struggle against include capitalism and the power of corporations.

In truth, I had been blind to Jesus's words about proclaiming good news to the poor and setting free the oppressed until I started reading books like these. Believers in the early church understood the need for sharing everything they had with their brothers and sisters (Acts 4:32–35). Now, many of us more closely resemble Ananias and Sapphira (Acts 5).

Capitalism need not be destroyed, as the Marxists argue, but it does need to be continually reformed to further social justice informed by kingdom principles.

Tastykake and Race

Many people think of the 1960s as a time when Martin Luther King Jr. helped the civil rights movement win greater equality for the nation's Blacks. But in the years before King brought attention to the civil rights movement, the victories were few, and many Blacks had to fight for the most basic element of economic equality.

I played a very small role in one victorious racial battle, and this experience changed my perspective on economic justice, showing me that people who were principled, passionate, and organized could do amazing things to level the economic playing field.

Philadelphia is home to the Tasty Baking Company, maker of the popular cake snack Tastykake. In the 1960s, the company employed Blacks, but only in lower-level, lower-paying positions. One of the most coveted positions was the driver-salesman position, which offered commissions on the sales that drivers made to vendors. Tasty Baking Company only hired white workers for this plum job.

When some people came to me to complain about the injustice of this prejudice, I connected them with Leon Howard Sullivan, a godly pastor who came to Philadelphia from Harlem in 1950 to lead Zion Baptist Church, a historic Black Baptist church, founded in 1882. The church had a reputation for being active in the community, and Sullivan carried on that tradition. Pastor Sullivan was an advocate of self-help for improving the lives of Black citizens, and he wrote *Build, Brother, Build: From Poverty to Economic Power* (1969).

Sullivan took up the issues at Tasty Baking with a group he had formed called the 400 Ministers. The pastors discussed the issue before deciding to give the company a series of demands for its Black employees. After the company rejected these demands, the 400 Ministers issued a call for a boycott. The boycott was based on campaigns Blacks had waged in the South on the principle of "Don't Buy Where You Can't Work."

Some individuals opposed the idea because Tastykake was an inexpensive treat that they enjoyed, but they joined the boycott under pressure from their pastors. Then the waiting began. "People want to see whether the Negro community will be strong enough to stand together in a cause that we know is right," said one leader.

Black-owned grocery stores refused to sell any Tasty Baking goods, and many posted signs announcing their support of the boycott. Tasty Baking fought back with a big public-relations campaign. But two months after the boycott started, the company gave in and agreed to the 400 Ministers' demands.

I was excited to see how people power could make capitalism work better and more fairly. (I was also grateful to be able to eat Tastykake once again because it is quite wonderful.) I played only a minor role in this protest, but through it I got to know the remarkable Leon Sullivan, and we remained friends until his death in 2001. This hometown victory prepared me to take on an even bigger target, a global, multibillion-dollar corporation that was abusing the people of the Dominican Republic.

The Sour Taste of Sugar

On April 28, 1965, President Lyndon Johnson sent twenty-two thousand troops to the Dominican Republic to prevent the establishment of a government Johnson called a "communist dictatorship." The United States had long engaged in gunboat diplomacy in Latin America, using its superior military force to change the politics of numerous countries, often installing anticommunist leaders who were also brutal and antidemocratic. Not wanting the Dominican Republic to go the way of communist Cuba, America installed a new government that was friendly to American political and economic interests.

In 1967, the multinational corporation Gulf+Western bought the South Puerto Rico Sugar Company, which controlled vast sugar plantations in the eastern half of the Dominican Republic. Gulf+Western kept expenses and salaries low so it could maximize profits, which reached $64 million in 1974 and 1975. But while the operation was good for Gulf+Western's bottom line, it was bad for workers.

This situation may never have landed on my radar if I had not visited the Dominican Republic as part of my work with EAPE. I had seen firsthand the poverty and lack of schools and hospitals in the eastern side of the country under Gulf+Western's control.

One day I was discussing Gulf+Western's harmful capitalism with Eastern College students in a senior seminar, and one of them said, "Why don't we do something about this?"

That simple question was the beginning of a long and amazing journey.

Shareholder Protest

My students and I decided we would follow the example of a group of Catholic nuns, the Adrian Dominican Sisters, who work to hold corporations responsible for their actions by buying stock in corporations and then attending stockholder meetings to identify abuses and promote alternatives.

Ten students and I each bought one share of Gulf+Western stock, at $10 each, so we could attend the company's shareholders meeting in Dallas. Along with the Adrian Sisters, we sat through the entire meeting until the end, when the discussion turned to new business. That's when we stood up and expressed our concerns.

"Gulf+Western exercises significant control over the eastern half of the country," I said, "but that control has not helped the people. There are no dedicated medical services for the residents. Worse, land that local communities once used to grow their own food has now been taken over and used to grow more sugar and more profits. Today, we are here to ask our fellow shareholders to hold the company responsible for its actions and require it to help the people it is exploiting for its own profits."

Nobody took us up on our request, and the meeting's leaders quickly moved on to other, safer topics. My students were concerned that our efforts on behalf of economic justice would amount to nothing. But after the meeting, reporters in attendance interviewed us. They included our protest in their coverage of the shareholder meeting, which led to a slight decrease in the value of Gulf+Western stock. We knew we had drawn the attention of the corporation's top executives, but still, we feared that nothing would be done.

Two weeks later, I was in my office at Eastern when a call came in from Gulf+Western. To my surprise, it was Robert Morsett, the corporation's executive vice president of public relations. He wanted to talk to me and my students, and he invited us to meet him and Martin Davis, Gulf+Western's CEO, at the company's headquarters on Columbus Circle in New York City.

When five students and I made our way to his office, Morsett wanted to hear more about EAPE's work in the Dominican Republic and our concerns about Gulf+Western's practices there. We explained our concerns and provided numerous suggestions of ways that Gulf+Western could make an important difference in the region.

"I will get back to you," Morsett told us as we left. Once again, we were skeptical. Morsett and other company leaders had listened intently to our concerns and taken extensive notes on our talk, but they did not say what they were thinking.

A Major Change

The next time I heard from Morsett, things were different. "Tony, we are about to make some significant changes," he told me. "Can we set up a time for me to come to Eastern and make a presentation to your student body?"

My students and I worked with the administration to schedule a public event in which Morsett would lay out what the company would do. It was quite an announcement. As he went through his list, we realized that he was granting us everything we had requested and more. Gulf+Western chose to

- develop a medical program with Mt. Sinai Hospital of New York City to provide medical services for people throughout the eastern part of the Dominican Republic;

- invest in projects that would help the Dominican people, including a baseball stadium in San Pedro that was considered ludicrously expensive at the time, but turned out to be a wonderful investment (San Pedro has produced about thirty to forty players who play for Major League Baseball teams);
- create a center called Artisan's Nationale to develop the craft skills already evident among Dominicans and provide a world market for these goods;
- make loans available to people who wanted to launch businesses;
- invest in the University of San Pedro, which trains people in medicine, business, and law and now has ten thousand students enrolled (many other universities, including EAPE's National Evangelical University of the Dominican Republic, were developed thanks to the original contributions of Gulf+Western); and
- help with other schools, investments in infrastructure, and a return of agricultural land to residents who could use it to grow food for themselves instead of growing more sugar for export.

These were not empty words. Gulf+Western backed up its many claims with cash. "We are going to spend $100 million on this next year and in each of the four following years for a total of half a billion dollars," Morsett told the stunned and joyous students.

The executives at Gulf+Western understood that its undertakings were good corporate policy, as well as gratifying and fulfilling. Its employees in the Dominican Republic became enthusiastic about the company. They walked with pride among their fellow citizens and ended up becoming very loyal to the American-based company.

I wrote about these developments in two of my books—*Let Me Tell You a Story: Life Lessons from Unexpected Places and Unlikely People*, and *Revolution and Renewal: How Churches Are Saving Our Cities*.

Part-Time Activist

For someone like me, who essentially stumbled into activism, it was pretty exciting and gratifying to see a major corporation listen to my students and the Catholic sisters and do the right thing. I felt that we had thrown a little stone into a pond, and that stone had caused ripples to extend far across the surface of the water, to borrow Robert F. Kennedy's famous metaphor. I thanked God for hearing and answering our prayers.

I was also grateful that my students got the education of a lifetime in seeing the power of protest. From then on, whenever I went to speak in a poor or developing country, leaders wanted to know about what we had done in the Dominican Republic, so they could replicate it in their countries.

In a strange way, I felt as if I was using faith and economics to satisfy the missionary impulse my mother drilled into me when I was a kid. Now I was sharing in Christ's mission of proclaiming good news to the poor and working to free those who were oppressed.

Years later, *Baptists Today* asked me to explain this work. Here's what I said: "I'm a totally committed American, but I get people calling me a socialist and all kinds of things simply because I say it's not enough just to feed the poor; we've got to, in fact, change the political and economic structures that are creating poverty. That has caused me a great deal of difficulty."

Evangelicals are now as concerned about the poor as mainline churches have been—maybe even more so. The place where evangelicals differ from mainline churches is that they are willing to respond to the poor with charity, but they are not about to raise serious questions about political and economic structures in America that are creating poverty.

In the words of the late Dom Hélder Câmara, archbishop of Recife, Brazil: "When I fed the poor, they called me a saint; when I began to ask what made them poor, they called me a communist."

CHAPTER 22

RADICAL? YES. HERETICAL? NO.

Once Galileo pointed his powerful new telescope at the heavens, he could see that the Earth and planets revolved around the Sun. Unfortunately, the Catholic Church was committed to an ancient cosmology that taught the Earth was the center of the cosmos. The Roman Inquisition put Galileo on trial, concluding in 1633 that he was "vehemently suspect of heresy," placing him under house arrest, and forbidding him from promoting his theories for the rest of his life (he died in 1642). Protestant reformer Martin Luther, who disagreed with the Catholic Church about so many things, agreed with them on this point.

Fortunately for Galileo, he was not executed, like thousands of lesser-known heretics over the centuries in both Catholic and Protestant countries. The Spanish Inquisition executed its last heretic in 1826.

American evangelicals cannot legally execute the people they consider heretics, so they persecute them with disfellowshipping, whisper campaigns, lost speaking engagements, canceled book contracts, and public protests.

That's what happened to me after I was branded a heretic by a powerful Christian leader, all because I had offended a key member of the evangelical hierarchy: a major financial donor.

As *Christianity Today* and other media outlets reported, I am no heretic. But the damage was done. I was soon assailed by other Christian leaders who had allied themselves with the Republican Party and were absolutely opposed to gay rights or even treating gay people with respect. Just thinking about these events brings back a host of unhappy memories.

Wealthy and Powerful Friends Become Enemies

The wealthy man was one of the most committed believers I ever knew, with a powerful passion for missions. His wife was a gifted singer and musician with a passion for conservative politics. Together, they were well known for their devotion to Christ and their funding of many major ministries and evangelistic initiatives.

They visited Upper Merion Baptist Church while I was a pastor there. They heard me preach on the importance of missions and learned about our church's support for a large number of missionaries and evangelists around the world. They soon joined our congregation, and before long she was our church's choir director.

One day he approached me with an offer. He wanted to give the church $200,000, an impressive amount for a congregation with a $150,000 annual budget. But there was a catch. He wanted this additional money to support the missionaries he and his wife had supported over the years.

I thanked him for the generous offer but let him know that his proposal might not work, because Upper Merion carefully selected its missionaries and would not want to automatically adopt missionaries it had not chosen or vetted.

My response offended them, and they left our church within a week's time, leaving a gaping hole in both our budget and our music program. They joined another nearby church, where they stayed for a couple of years, before leaving to start a new church of their own.

I further offended the wife many years later, when I spoke at Wheaton College's Spiritual Vision Week and encouraged students to pursue God's will for their futures. Her daughter, who was a student there, apparently reported back to her mother that my talk had included a brief theological critique of capitalism. That offended them further, so they mounted a pressure campaign to make sure I wouldn't pollute any more young Christian minds.

That's what led to the Great Campolo Heresy Trials. As *Christianity Today* reported: "Campolo, one of the most traveled speakers on the evangelical circuit, became the center of a controversy earlier this year when he was canceled on theological grounds from speaking at Youth Congress '85 (CT, Sept. 20, 1985, p. 30). The decision was made by Bill Bright, president of Campus Crusade for Christ, one of the sponsoring organizations of the youth conference."[4]

I now had enemies. And not just any enemies—mine were powerful and influential funders of important Christian organizations that had previously been enthusiastic about offering important speaking opportunities to me, but now began to hesitate. It was not a coincidence. I was stunned. But even more stunning was the public accusation that followed, based on a conservative researcher's claim that one of my frequently used sermon illustrations smacked of heresy.

The Heresy Accusation

If you have ever heard me speak in support of Compassion International, World Vision, or Prison Fellowship, you have probably heard me tell some version of a story that I have told hundreds of times. I included this story in my 1983 book *A Reasonable Faith*.

I had visited a small community in Haiti near Cap Haitien and was standing at the edge of a grass landing strip awaiting the arrival of a Mission Aviation Fellowship plane that would pick me up and fly me to Santo Domingo, the capital city of the Dominican Republic.

As I waited for the plane, a woman came toward me carrying her baby boy. In an instant I could see the telltale signs of chronic malnutrition and illness. His stomach was swollen and distended. His spindly arms and legs hung limply from his semi-conscious body. His black hair had turned rust colored. I could see he was on his way to dying.

"Don't let my baby die," the woman pleaded, holding her son in front of me. "Please don't let him die. Take him and make him well again. Take him back to your country and make him your child. Feed him and make him well."

I tried to explain that I could not take her son, but she would not stop and kept begging me, grabbing at me and pulling on my clothes.

"Please take my baby!" she said again and again, even as I boarded the small plane. Left outside, she banged helplessly on the fuselage until the plane began to taxi down the grassy run-way. As we gained speed, she ran alongside with her sick baby for as long as she could, pleading and screaming in despair, until our plane rose up into the sky.

The pilot and I were both visibly shaken as we gained elevation and left the woman and her boy below. As we flew, I realized something. The malnourished boy I had left behind on that grass landing strip was more than another statistical victim of an oppressive economic system. That little boy was Jesus.

When I used the story in my talks, I explained why I saw things that way, citing Jesus's teaching on the sheep and the goats found in Matthew 25:31-46. Jesus praises the sheep for helping people like that little Haitian boy, making the story very personal: "Come, you who are blessed by my Father; take your inheritance, the kingdom prepared for you since the creation of the world. For I was hungry and you gave me something to eat, I was thirsty and you gave me something to drink, I was a stranger and you invited me in, I needed clothes and you clothed me, I was sick and you looked after me, I was in prison and you came to visit me."

But his listeners were confused and asked Jesus to clarify what he meant about the sheep and goats. Why did Jesus say that giving food to a hungry man was giving food to Jesus?

"Lord, when did we see you hungry and feed you, or thirsty and give you something to drink? When did we see you a stranger and invite you in, or needing clothes and clothe you? When did we see you sick or in prison and go to visit you?"

Jesus explained: "Truly I tell you, whatever you did for one of the least of these brothers and sisters of mine, you did for me."

"Lord, when did we see you hungry or thirsty or a stranger or needing clothes or sick or in prison, and did not help you?"

Jesus said, "Truly I tell you, whatever you did not do for one of the least of these, you did not do for me."

The point of this story and the source of its message are very clear. But to my amazement, I learned that I was now being accused of committing heresy for my application of Jesus's words to that dying Haitian boy. I was being called a universalist—someone who believes that all humans will be saved and go to heaven—even though I did not believe in universal salvation then and do not believe in it today.

I would soon receive a phone call.

"Tony, can you come out to California to see if we can resolve this matter?"

Red Lion Inn, Anaheim, May 8, 1985

I flew to California for a meeting with the two men who led the two big youth ministries that were teaming up to organize Youth Congress '85. This would be the first time I met Bill Bright, but I had been close friends for years with Jay Kessler, who led Youth for Christ.

"Tony, if Bill could just hear you out personally, this whole conflict could be settled," Jay told me. I hoped Jay's optimism would win out, but I knew that Bright faced continuing pressure to exclude me from the Youth Congress roster.

The gathering took on a prosecutorial tone as Professor Randy Rodden's thirty-five-page analysis of my heresies was argued by Randy's brother, Dan.

When I had a chance to talk, I shared my personal testimony of faith in Christ and described what Jesus meant to me. I explicitly denied the charge of teaching universalism and discussed the Holy Spirit's role in bringing us to Christ.

"I did not claim the Haitian boy was a Christian, or equal to Christ," I said. "I don't know anything about his soul or beliefs. I simply said about him what Christ said about the hungry, the thirsty, and the naked people Jesus was teaching us to serve. Christ said he was somehow mystically present in those needy people, and I applied that teaching to one little boy."

I discussed the Holy Spirit's role in conversion, moving in every person to bring them toward Christ, even when people have no interest in or knowledge of Christ.

But my testimony did not carry the day. The upshot of the meeting was that I was now perceived as a person whose views and statements might pose a threat to the faith of other Christians. Immediately, the planners of a huge youth rally at which I'd been invited to speak suddenly felt compelled to withdraw their invitation. For the first time in my life, I experienced the unpleasant phenomenon of being canceled. Of course, the cynic in me could not resist connecting the dots between my cancellation and the rally's dependence on my wealthy enemies' substantial financial support.

I was sad and angry about what had happened. But I was also worried, as it soon became clear that the campaign to cancel me would not end with the youth rally. To the contrary, it seemed to be just beginning. But what could I do?

Out of the Blue

One day I received an unexpected call from Charles Colson, who had been part of Nixon's criminal Watergate gang, went to prison, came to Christ, founded Prison Fellowship, and then served as a roving evangelical bridge-builder and peacemaker.

"Tony, I hear you're being condemned as a heretic."

"Tell me something I don't know," I said.

"Well, if you are being accused of heresy, why don't you demand a heresy trial?"

"How in the world would I do that?"

"Leave it to me," he assured me. "I'll organize it."

And that is how I came to face the unlikely ordeal of a heresy trial, as an American evangelical in the twentieth century.

The Great Chicago Heresy Trial

Colson got to work, lining up the Christian Legal Society to help organize my trial, which was held in December 1985 at a hotel at Chicago's O'Hare International Airport.

The official chairman of the proceedings was esteemed evangelical theologian J. I. Packer, who taught at Regent College in Vancouver, was an editor for *Christianity Today*, and wrote the bestselling book *Knowing God*.

The jury included three respected Christian leaders: Gordon MacDonald, president of InterVarsity Christian Fellowship; Earl Radmacher, president of Western Conservative Baptist Seminary; and James Boice, pastor of Tenth Presbyterian Church in Philadelphia and a well-known Christian radio celebrity.

Christianity Today reported on the meeting:

> Packer said the panel's purpose was limited, explaining that it had been summoned as part of a process to reconcile Campolo with his critics.
>
> "Our goal was to produce a resource document to help the parties in this case to achieve reconciliation."
>
> At the one-day meeting in Chicago, the panel questioned Campolo for a total of six hours, calling on him to explain parts of *A Reasonable Faith*, which . . . [was] cited as the basis for . . . [the] cancellation of Campolo.[5]

The jurors took time to deliberate before releasing their verdict. As *Christianity Today* reported: "A panel of evangelical leaders has determined that Tony Campolo cannot rightly be called a heretic. However, the panel urged the Eastern College sociology professor to clarify in writing certain statements made in his book, *A Reasonable Faith*. The panel said the book is 'methodologically naïve and verbally incautious.'"

The jury concluded that when I said Christ was present in the poor and oppressed, I had taken the Bible too literally. This is a charge typically made against fundamentalists, and not "liberal" evangelicals like me.

Canceled

I had won, but I had still lost. The verdict of my innocence effectively countered the claims that I was a heretic, but it could not erase the damage those claims had caused—and would continue to cause—to me, my career, and the ministries that depended on me to help them raise the funds they needed to do their work.

These days, one can hear conservative Christians decrying "cancel culture," claiming it's a liberal plot to silence them. But anyone can cancel someone else, and in this case my conservative Christian brothers had canceled me.

At some of my speaking engagements that were not canceled, picketers and protesters showed up to express their disapproval. I was speaking to raise funds and awareness for a rescue mission serving the urban poor of Milwaukee when some of my critics let themselves into the mission's men's dorm, stuffed rolls of toilet paper into the toilets, flushed the toilets, and sent water cascading all over the dorm's floor.

One Southern Baptist leader from Texas wrote me a letter saying that I did not deserve the grace of God. I wrote him back, saying he was right. "None of us deserve God's grace," I wrote. "Grace is his loving gift to us, a gift we are commanded to share with others."

From Condemnation to Liberation

If people thought a heresy accusation and trial would shut me up, they had another think coming. I took the Chicago jury's comments seriously. I thought long and hard on those words—"methodologically naïve and verbally incautious"—and committed myself to greater rigor in articulating my thoughts with more theological precision in the years ahead.

I did not stop exercising my calling to apply orthodox Christian teaching to the challenges of the present, but my venues and audiences changed.

I was heartbroken to be cut off from groups of young people I had addressed for years, but other groups welcomed me with open arms, including Quakers, who teach believers to walk in the light of Christ, which is his presence in every person.

In the end, Bill Bright met with me privately and offered me his sincere and personal apology for the whole mess. I forgave him without reservation.

While some evangelical churches and ministries dropped me, my persecution made me a hero among more theologically and politically progressive Christians. My victory in a bad-faith heresy trial granted me bragging rights that increased my allure in nonevangelical circles. I even made the cover of *The Door*, a witty magazine published by Youth Specialties, which gave the heresy trial wall-to-wall coverage.

My theology was not changing, but my public image was, because my audience now skewed more liberal—a perception that would only grow once it became public knowledge that I was a spiritual confidant of President Bill Clinton.

When I got over feeling canceled and condemned, I began to feel liberated. Plus, my crucible gave me new topics I could present in my talks:

- "The power of money in evangelical churches and parachurch organizations." I certainly had plenty of fresh stories showing how wealth buys influence in the nation's most influential ministries.
- "The marriage between American evangelicalism and the Republican Party."
- "Freezing them out: how to cancel opposing views."

Lasting Legacy

This whole crazy conflict changed my life, and I sometimes wonder if it did not also have a chilling effect on evangelicals seeking to engage the broader intellectual world outside our community and its self-appointed gatekeepers.

As I told *Christianity Today* in a special issue featuring three separate articles on my heresy trial: "I'm worried that evangelical intellectuals will not say anything except the old phrases and the old worn-out terminology. . . . The way evangelical Christianity is doing theology really bothers me. If everybody has to say only things that they know are safely orthodox, if we lose the capacity to be open and to share ideas that people may consider heretical, I think we will lose our creativity."

Eventually, I came to see my heresy trial as a badge of honor. I told my fellow evangelicals: "As a result of having been tried and tested and judged by a jury of evangelical leaders, I have officially been declared an evangelical. None of the rest of you can say that."

CHAPTER 23

CLINTONISTA

The phone call came in January 1993. Would I be willing to meet for breakfast with newly elected President Bill Clinton and a few other Christian leaders? At first, I thought it might be a prank, but the professionalism and seriousness of the call allayed my fears.

"I would be privileged," I said. I was not sure what wisdom I could provide. But as a Christian and an American, I believed that the only appropriate response to a presidential summons was a quick "Yes, sir!"

I would have said the same thing if a Republican president called me, but the fact that I was a Democrat who had run for Congress in 1976 and voted for Clinton made my answer easier.

Thus began my decades-long relationship with Bill Clinton, which turned into an improbable friendship that continues to this day. Our relationship enabled me to offer faith-based policy ideas at the highest levels of national policy, involved me in intense discussions about his sex scandal and an impeachment attempt, subjected me to unprecedented levels of media scrutiny, and brought even more complaints about me from conservative evangelicals who had hitched their faith to the Republican Party.

From Bitter Baptists to Loving Leaders

President Clinton and Vice President Al Gore, both lifelong Southern Baptists, received a visit from a group of Southern Baptist leaders shortly after winning the election. But these leaders were not interested in congratulating their brothers in Christ or discussing ways they could work together.

Instead, they condemned the new administration over its support for abortion and gay rights, and then bragged about their condemnation from their pulpits and on Christian radio shows. (At the Southern Baptist Convention's June 1993 convention, leaders introduced nineteen resolutions criticizing Clinton and Gore. Two motions calling for withdrawing fellowship with the men were ruled out of order, but the resolution calling on Clinton and Gore to "repent of leading our nation in a direction that is unbiblical, unwise, and offensive to God" easily passed.)

The meeting frustrated Clinton's efforts to work with faith groups, so Linda Lader, his liaison to the evangelical community, suggested she organize a group of leaders he could talk with constructively, without fear of being hounded or misquoted in the press. Phone calls soon went out to World Vision president Bob Seiple; *Christianity Today* editor David Neff; Fuller Theological Seminary president Richard Mouw; American Bible Society president Eugene Habecker; John Perkins, founder of Voice of Calvary; and me.

When we met with the president and vice president for breakfast in January, President told us he wanted to hear our ideas on how churches and government could work together to address problems that afflict urban populations, including poverty, unemployment, addiction, and crime. As we talked together, I was in awe of the privilege I had to engage the president of the United States about substantial policy matters that intersected with the commands of Scripture to care for "the least of these."

Clinton had just launched the AmeriCorps National Service Trust to promote public service. I urged him to make sure that AmeriCorps volunteers could volunteer with religious organizations.

I also mentioned the case of a group of women who had been holding Bible studies at an apartment in Bartram Village in Philadelphia. The housing was operated by the Department of Housing and Urban Development (HUD). A HUD official reportedly told the women that their Bible study was not permitted on federal property.

The next day, administration officials called my office at Eastern to get more details, which impressed the entire staff. Following a few more calls, we received a report: the president had asked staff members to look into the problem, and they called the relevant parties and made a "correction," allowing the Bible studies to continue.

I also had a chance to encourage Clinton after his brutal run-in with the Southern Baptist leaders. I assured him that not all Christians saw things the way his Southern Baptist critics did. I told him that I appreciated that he was treating the gay and lesbian community with decency and respect and that I was not the only follower of Jesus who felt that way.

He thanked me and asked me to contact him whenever I was in Washington. I assumed this was mere presidential gladhanding, not a sincere request, and gave it little thought. But I soon found out he was serious.

Summoned to the Oval Office

A week or so later, I was speaking at a church in Washington when the church secretary approached me in the middle of my talk. I paused my talk for a moment as she whispered into my ear: "The President of the United States is on the phone and says he wants to speak with you," she whispered to me. "I think this is for real!"

I abruptly ended my talk and rushed to the phone to see what the problem was.

It was indeed President Clinton. To my astonishment, he had seen in the newspaper that I was speaking at a local church, and he chided me for not contacting him to let him know I was in town.

"I'm sorry, Mr. President," I said, a bit flummoxed. "I didn't quite know what to do. Am I just supposed to call the White House and say, 'Hello, this is Tony Campolo and I want to speak to the president?'"

He said that was *exactly* what I was supposed to do. So, I promptly left the church and headed over to the White House, where the president and I spent nearly an hour talking, as always including spiritual topics. And I promised the president that I would do better next time and let him know when I was in D.C. again. As we discussed what the Bible says about the role of government, I pointed him to Paul's teaching on principalities and powers: "Put on the full armor of God, so that you can take your stand against the devil's schemes. For our struggle is not against flesh and blood, but against the rulers, against the authorities, against the powers of this dark world and against the spiritual forces of evil in the heavenly realms" (Eph. 6:11–12).

As he explained his vision for how churches could serve as agents of positive social change, especially in the inner city, I shared with the president how excited I was about the powerful transformation our ministry, EAPE, and students at Eastern were seeing in the lives of poor people being transformed through microloans. Through small loans made to impoverished people, we helped them buy hogs for breeding, sewing machines to make alterations, and other purchases that brought them income and employed others nearby.

He listened attentively to what I said, and his later administration offered microloans to small businesses in the United States. The administration would also work with the ministry Opportunity International to expand its microloan program.

Prayer Breakfasts and Renaissance Weekends

Over the next couple of years, I would see the president regularly at public gatherings. In time I grew close to his staff and even performed a marriage ceremony for his personal secretary.

In February 1993, Peggy and I attended the annual National Prayer Breakfast. When we arrived, a Clinton aide said, "Wait right here. The president wants to talk to you." Clinton soon said hello to the two of us, telling us about his deep involvement in Baptist churches and about how he used to travel with an evangelist and play saxophone during meetings. He also commented on a simple little frog pin that Peggy wore on her dress, something he brought up time and time again in years to come.

Peggy asked me later why a man with the weight of the world on his shoulders could comment on what she wore while her husband largely overlooked such niceties. Bill was unusually gifted in the kind of attention he paid to people. When you talked with him, you had the feeling that there was nobody else in the whole world he was thinking about but you.

We also ran into the Clintons at Renaissance Weekends, a retreat in which leaders from many fields exchange ideas about policy and economics. I was invited to give a talk to a dinner meeting about the three things I would do differently if I could do it all over again. I adopted the top three choices made by a group of elderly people who were surveyed on the subject:

- Risk more.
- Reflect more.
- Do more things that will live on after I'm dead.

As usual, I illustrated my points with insights from sociology and Scripture.

People applauded politely, but apparently the response was not enough for the president, who stood up, applauded energetically, and persuaded everyone else to join him in a standing ovation.

Soon after, he was saying that I was one of his favorite preachers, and he began contacting me for my thoughts about navigating conflicts in the evangelical subculture. I felt like some kind of unofficial advisor. I would raise questions about what he was doing and where he was leading the country, as a Christian should.

One holiday season, he read to me some of the remarks he planned to make at the lighting of the White House Christmas tree. I stopped him when he referred to the "magic" of Christmas and pointed out that some evangelicals would associate that word with witchcraft.

At the 1994 Renaissance Weekend, with the president in the audience, I spoke about the work EAPE was doing in inner cities. My comments inspired a surprising addition to his next State of the Union address. Peggy and I were watching his speech on TV on the evening of January 25, 1994, when we heard him make this unexpected addition to his scripted remarks:

"We can't renew our country unless more of us, I mean all of us, are willing to join churches and the other good citizens, people like all the—like ministers I've worked with over the years or the priests and the nuns I met at Our Lady of Help in East Los Angeles or my good friend Tony Campolo in Philadelphia."

I nearly fell out of my chair, and in seconds, our phone answering machine filled with congratulatory calls.

Meanwhile, Dee Dee Myers, the president's press secretary, was asking the question that others in the Capitol were probably also asking:

"Who the hell is Tony Campolo?"

I was thrilled.

President Clinton wanted help in developing speeches, so I became an occasional consultant for his speechwriters whenever they needed input on matters that touched on religion.

The president was scheduled to travel to Oklahoma City to speak at the dedication of a memorial to the victims of the massive bombing of the Alfred P. Murrah Federal Building. When a speech was drafted, the president asked for my thoughts.

"You're an old-time Southern Baptist," I told him. "What if you ended your talk with a quote from an old gospel song?"

I had a particular gospel song in mind, and I recommended these words from "Farther Along" by W. B. Stevens, a song the president recognized:

> Farther along we'll know all about it,
> Farther along we'll understand why;
> Cheer up, don't worry, live in the sunshine,
> We'll understand it all by and by.

I smiled when I learned that the president did in fact include those lyrics in his address.

Lewinsky Scandal Changes Everything

President Clinton easily won reelection in 1996 with 49 percent of the popular vote, compared to 41 percent for Republican Senator Bob Dole and 8 percent for independent candidate Ross Perot.

He invited me to deliver the sermon at a prayer breakfast celebrating his second term, and I was honored to do so. The event was held at a Black church near the Capitol, and I spoke about how both the president and vice president had talked with me about their desire to take care of the poor. The sermon was carried live on some TV networks, leading to my appearances on *Nightline*, *Larry King Live*, *Good Morning America*, and *PBS NewsHour*.

As the world knows, Clinton's second term was upended by the scandal of an affair with a White House intern named Monica Lewinsky. News about the affair broke in January 1998. By the end of that year, Clinton was charged with lying under oath and obstructing justice and was impeached by the House of Representatives. But at the trial in the Senate, Republicans joined with forty-five Senate Democrats to acquit the president, and Clinton served out the rest of his second term. While damaged politically, he continued to seek spiritual strength and healing.

Assembling a Pastoral Team

I got a call from the president shortly before the independent counsel Kenneth Starr released his lengthy report on Clinton to Congress, and after hearing from the president, I prayed: "Lord, show me what to say. Help me be strong and faithful to the truth so that I will not be intimidated by the power and trimmings of the presidency." Then I got on the phone. I began seeking fellow Christian leaders who could meet with Clinton and walk with him through his mess.

Gordon MacDonald was part of the group of Christian leaders who met with Clinton in his first term. He is a respected former pastor, author, and ministry leader who was involved in an adulterous relationship and stepped down from his roles in 1987, sought healing and forgiveness for his sins, and later returned to ministry. I recommended him, knowing he could serve as a confessor while also helping the president deal with the spiritual and psychological issues of the affair.

The third member of our advisory trio was J. Philip Wogaman, pastor of Foundry United Methodist Church in Washington. He was the Clintons' pastor.

My role was to help the president understand what he had to do spiritually to hold his marriage together and repent of his sin. During this time, I talked to Mrs. Clinton as well and found her to be very knowledgeable about Scripture.

She remained committed to restoring the marriage, a theme she touched on during her New York Senate campaign when she was criticized by feminists for staying with an adulterous husband.

"You have to understand that when I married Bill, I promised to stay with him for better, or for worse, till death do us part," she told one crowd. "I keep my promises that I made to the president, and if you elect me senator from New York, I will keep all the promises I made to you as well."

Repentance

I had to give advice that was not easy to give to the president of the United States, including a mini-sermon on the importance of confession of and repentance from sin. President Clinton listened and heard me, and he also consulted with a number of other religious leaders, including pastors, rabbis, Buddhist teachers, and imams. On September 11, 1998, he delivered a famous speech at the annual National Prayer Breakfast. Here is part of what he said:

> I may not be quite as easy with my words today as I have been in years past, and I was up rather late last night thinking about and praying about what I ought to say today. And rather unusual for me, I actually tried to write it down. So, if you will forgive me, I will do my best to say what it is I want to say to you.
>
> I agree with those who have said that in my first statement after I testified I was not contrite enough. I don't think there is a fancy way to say that I have sinned.
>
> It is important to me that everybody who has been hurt knows that the sorrow I feel is genuine: first and most important, my family; also, my friends, my staff, my Cabinet, Monica Lewinsky and her family, and the American people. I have asked all for their forgiveness.

> But I believe that to be forgiven, more than sorrow is required—at least two more things. First, genuine repentance—a determination to change and to repair breaches of my own making. I have repented. Second, what my Bible calls a "broken spirit"; an understanding that I must have God's help to be the person that I want to be; a willingness to give the very forgiveness I seek; a renunciation of the pride and the anger which cloud judgment, lead people to excuse and compare and to blame and complain.
>
> I will continue on the path of repentance, seeking pastoral support and that of other caring people so that they can hold me accountable for my own commitment.
>
> In this, I ask for your prayers and for your help in healing our nation. And though I cannot move beyond or forget this—indeed, I must always keep it as a caution light in my life—it is very important that our nation move forward.

The president also announced that he was being helped by a group of Christian leaders. He did not name us, but the media would soon find out who we were.

Outed and Hassled

The *New York Times* broke the news, identifying the three of us who were meeting with the president.[6] Once again, Christian leaders who had allied themselves with the Republican Party assailed me. The president of the Christian Booksellers Association threatened to ban my books from thousands of Christian bookstores.

For decades, Billy Graham loyally served twelve presidents, both Republicans and Democrats, beginning with Harry Truman in 1950 and continuing through Barack Obama. He was admired for doing so, even though each one of those twelve presidents, like everyone else on this earth, was a sinner in need of forgiveness and grace. But amid the growing power of the religious right, I was being condemned for providing spiritual guidance to one of those presidents.

President Clinton invited me to be with him at the White House on February 12, 1999, the day the Senate would vote to acquit him of the charges brought by the House. We spent a good part of the morning praying together, and I was proud to be able to support him in a moment of need. After the Senate's verdict, I thought our weekly meetings with the president might tail off, but we continued meeting throughout his second term, which ended in January 2001.

As he prepared to leave office, I assumed once again that our relationship would probably end, but he continued to quietly seek guidance on his spiritual journey long after the glare of publicity subsided. Strange as it may seem, and despite the unlikely and difficult circumstances, we became and have remained friends.

CHAPTER 24

THE PRODIGAL SON

My work as a teacher, author, public speaker, and counselor to a president made me a public theologian—someone who does theology in the public sphere, not in academia's ivory towers. I loved theologizing with the masses, but the downside of being a public theologian is that even private, personal matters can become fodder for public debate.

That was the case after my son, Bart, left the Christian faith to become something that evangelicals have long condemned: a secular humanist. Because Bart and I both ministered in public, this was a news story that was reported by both the religious and secular media. News stories led my more conservative Christian brethren to offer new criticisms.

"So, how does it feel to know your son is going to hell?" asked one man in a crank phone message.

I do not believe Bart is going to hell, for reasons I will explain, but the whole situation sure made me feel as if I was already in some kind of hell.

Thanksgiving Revelation

Bart and his wife, Marty, invited Peggy and me to spend Thanksgiving 2014 with them at their home in Cincinnati. After a wonderful dinner and time together, Bart said there was something he wanted to talk to us about. He took us back to their bedroom and closed the door as Peggy and I sat together on the bed, uncertain about what was coming our way. Then he dropped the bomb.

Bart told us he no longer believed in God. Long story short: his faith in Christ, which he affirmed when he was a sophomore in high school, had been eroded by growing doubts over many years. Then in 2011, a horrible bicycle accident left Bart hospitalized, caused a serious head injury, and made him rethink his life in the light of this close brush with mortality.

I was shocked—if not completely surprised—and heartbroken. It felt as if Bart was not only rejecting the Christian faith but also rejecting me, as well as the faith I had built my life and career around.

Bart said he was not rejecting God, or Jesus, or Christianity, or me. "It's just that none of this stuff is real to me anymore," he said.

"You talk about having a personal relationship with Jesus like he's right here in the room with you," Bart told me. "You can talk to him and feel like he interacts with you. But I don't feel his presence."

God calls parents to pass on the faith to the next generation. As the King James Version puts it, "Train up a child in the way he should go: and when he is old, he will not depart from it" (Prov. 22:6). I have always believed that as father and husband I should lead my family into an ever-deepening life of following Jesus Christ. My parents had passed on the faith to me, and it stuck. Now I felt as if I had failed in my duty as a Christian father to pass on the faith to my son. The chain of faith apparently had a weak link. I felt like a failure as a father and a disciple of Christ.

Paul's words in 1 Timothy 3:5 rang in my ears and reproached me for my failings: "If anyone does not know how to manage his own family, how can he take care of God's church?"

There was a sharp irony to it all. I was famous for preaching to hundreds of thousands of young people, introducing as many as I could to Jesus, and challenging them to serve him with their lives. But my son would choose a different path.

Our Family's Faith Journey

"Raising our children to hold onto a living faith is nearly guaranteed," wrote Glenn Stanton, a culture specialist with Focus on the Family. "It's relatively simple, and any parent can do it." That's what I experienced, growing up in a family infused by my mother's powerful faith. But that's not what happened when I tried to raise Lisa and Bart in the love of the Lord.

I have often wondered how that could be and wished I fully understood. One challenge was that I was often gone. My speaking schedule often took me from home and left me unable to be the husband and father I needed to be. My regular absences also meant that I did not lead my family's Sunday church attendance, and my behavior may have unintentionally signaled that family church attendance was not a priority.

Another challenge was that Peggy and I were not always on the same page spiritually. Peggy spent many years of our married life doubting her faith, until the day came when she had a personal experience with Jesus.

As she says, "What I deeply regret is that that day came far too late for my children to have been raised by a truly authentic Christian mother."

From the beginning, I would take Lisa and Bart with me on some of my speaking engagements. I do not think Lisa ever liked these events very much, but Bart seemed more interested.

Nor did Lisa have much interest in the family devotions and Bible readings I organized. She would occasionally tease me for my bibliocentric approach to life, lifting a forefinger toward heaven and piously declaring, with a smile, "Verily, verily, I say to you." At times, Peggy would join her in ribbing me.

In high school, Lisa became close friends with two Jewish girls. One night she came to me in some distress and asked if I believed her friends were going to hell. I was amazed to see her wrestling with the same question that I also asked back in high school when a group of smart, loving, and devoted Jewish friends helped my church's basketball team. Because this was a question I had struggled with as a teenager, I felt well-equipped to respond, and I shared my understanding with her, which I could see brought her some comfort.

I wanted Bart and Lisa to attend Christian colleges, but neither of them was interested in that. They were both particularly determined not to attend Eastern, where they knew they would be seen as the teacher's kids. Both attended intellectually demanding secular colleges where both of them majored in religion. They were asking all the right questions, but I lacked adequate answers for them, and I saw their doubts being amplified by their secular college courses.

Lisa has gone on to enjoy a wonderful life. She married an amazing man and has two terrific kids, and she has enjoyed a successful career as a lawyer. I am proud of her values and her commitment to public service. Some people have asked Peggy, "How did you feel about your daughter marrying a Jewish man?" Peggy's response was classic: "If you had known some of the Christians she dated, you would understand why I kiss the ground this man walks on."

Bart, too, has made Peggy and me proud in many ways. He married a wonderful woman and has two incredible children, who in turn have great spouses and beautiful children of their own. He works as a professional counselor, and his core commitment is to help people build great relationships, cultivate wonder, and make things better for other people. Peggy and I feel blessed that our children are living good lives, and we are grateful that they have internalized good values. Despite our spiritual differences, which do pain me, we are a close and loving family.

In Praise of Plausibility Structures

Unlike Lisa, who is a skeptic by nature and always has been, Bart seemed open and receptive to Jesus and Christian principles for most of his life. Growing up, he was so kind, considerate, and caring that Peggy occasionally thought he had been "Christian from birth." But he was not, and sociology can help explain his journey.

Sociologists Peter Berger and Thomas Luckman blew my mind with their 1966 book, *The Social Construction of Reality: A Treatise in the Sociology of Knowledge.* They described how the social groups that you and I join and nurture provide us with plausibility structures that help us make sense of the world.

My family of origin gave me a plausibility structure that helped me make sense of Christianity and accept it for myself. This plausibility structure grew even stronger at church, where many other people testified to the truth of the faith we all embraced. And when I connected with the Bible Buzzards, I was drawn even more deeply into a faith community that adopted a particular worldview and code of conduct.

Forces like these mold and influence our lives in powerful ways. Fortunately, I had something even more powerful than socially constructed realities: I had a personal relationship with Jesus Christ that transformed me and empowered me.

As a teenager, Bart's involvement in Salt, a youth group at the Church of the Saviour in Wayne, Pennsylvania, led to his own "on fire for Jesus" period, which bore a striking resemblance to my youthful fundamentalism. But later, Bart said he never really experienced a connection with Christ, but only the plausibility structures and social networks that were built up around Christian activities. He latched onto a series of social groups that allowed him to construct a pseudo-Christian social reality that survived until his growing doubts caught up with him.

In my teaching and speaking, I had often encountered college students and other young people who told me such stories about loss of faith, but it was different to hear such an account from my son. I struggled to understand what was happening in his heart.

Doing His Father's Work

"Dear Dad: You are an incredibly tough act to follow. Whenever I compare myself to you, I come out the loser, Dad, and yet, more and more as I get older, I can't stop myself from doing it all the same. I think you are a great father. Having said that, though, I still need to answer the question of what it means to be your son."

These words are from Bart's opening chapter in the book he and I wrote together way back in 1989, *Things We Wish We Had Said: Reflections of a Father and His Grown Son.*

After years of being introduced as "Tony's kid," Bart developed a life and career of his own. Ironically, he eventually became a Christian celebrity in his own right by doing the kinds of things he had seen me doing from the time he was born. He became a popular speaker whose talks could move a small church group or a field full of thirty thousand young people. He and his wife, Marty, created Mission Year, a Christian organization that served the poor in Philadelphia, Chicago, Atlanta, and Oakland.

Bart was committed to ministry and was already booked for a number of future speaking and fundraising events when he began having serious doubts about his faith. For a while, he continued doing Christian work because it supported his family and was the only work he knew. But his cognitive dissonance was growing, and in time he publicly admitted that he was not a believer anymore.

Peggy and I both respect him for his honesty and integrity. People praise those who bravely stand up for their faith. Bart showed the same bravery in standing up for his doubt.

Media Spread the News

Speakers, pastors, authors, theologians, musicians, youth workers, and those who serve Christ as "public Christians" owe it to the public to be transparent and honest. Are they sincere believers serving Christ, or hucksters trying to make a quick buck on the God market?

As much as I hated the intrusion, I understood that the public had a right to know about Bart's loss of faith. I was not surprised that the news media, both Christian and secular, covered Bart's journey away from Christ and his later work as a humanist college chaplain.

Jonathan Merritt of Religion News Service was the first to report on Bart's loss of faith. He gave a road map of Bart's journey of doubt:

> His first step away from orthodoxy occurred while doing inner-city ministry near Philadelphia. Bart encountered a girl who had been gang-raped at age 9 and who rejected Christianity after her Sunday school teacher said God could have stopped the act but allowed it for a reason.
>
> Bart decided that if he was going to remain a Christian, he had to believe that God did not authorize that child's rape and was not in control of the world. He began to imagine God as engaged in a battle with good and evil rather than a cosmic marionette pulling the universe's strings.
>
> The next rejection occurred as a student at Haverford College in 1981, when two of Bart's roommates came out to him as gay. Though evangelical Christian teachings repudiated same-sex orientation at the time, he chose instead to jettison the biblical verses that spoke negatively of homosexuality.[7]

Another factor for Bart was seeing how conservative Christians condemned me for my social positions on war and capitalism. Bart came along with me to the California meeting at which I met with one of the conservative evangelicals who had called me a heretic. The meeting did not go well. At one point, my critic turned to my son and said, "Bart, I hope this conversation doesn't cause you any disillusionment about the evangelical world." Bart replied with honesty: "I don't see why it shouldn't."

In the wake of Bart's public announcement about his loss of faith, the *New York Times* followed up with a story that followed Bart's journey to his new career as a humanist chaplain at the University of Southern California (USC). Bart missed the connections he experienced in Christian circles, and he worked to create a new community of student nonbelievers on the USC campus.[8]

Almost a Universalist?

Today Bart works in Cincinnati as a family and marriage counselor, helping people save and strengthen broken relationships. The two of us have spent a lot of time trying to find the best way to relate as father and son, now that we are no longer on the same page spiritually. Because there had been so much media coverage of what happened, we decided to tell the story ourselves in a 2017 DVD, *Leaving My Father's Faith*, and a 2018 book, *Why I Left, Why I Stayed*. The interactions captured in our video and book probably provide more insight into our journey as father and son than either of us can offer on our own.

Meanwhile, Peggy and I consider Bart a disciple of Jesus, if not a believer, because of the work he does and the Christlike way in which he does it. In some ways, he is like Mahatma Gandhi, the revered Indian leader who implemented the teachings of Jesus in his life but never became a confessing Christian.

Peggy compares Bart to St. Francis, citing this quote often attributed to Francis: "Preach the gospel at all times, and when necessary, use words." Peggy believes Bart is doing God's work, even if he does not use or even believe the God language he once embraced. And she agrees with me that, in many ways, unbelieving Bart is a better Christian than his Jesus-preaching dad.

I still believe that Jesus is the only way to salvation, but I do not believe that Christians are the only people Jesus will save. I take comfort in the words of Jesus, who said, "I have other sheep that are not of this sheep pen. I must bring them also. They too will listen to my voice, and there shall be one flock and one shepherd" (John 10:16).

Some people say this makes me a universalist, but I am not, at least not entirely. I have one core belief that disqualifies me from that title. I still believe in God's judgment and hell, and I believe people go to hell through their choices, not because God likes punishing people, but because divine justice demands that evil be punished.

CHAPTER 25

RED LETTER CHRISTIANS

People first heard about the religious right in the 1970s, when conservative Christians battling gay rights claimed to be speaking in God's name as they portrayed homosexuals as sickly perverts out to recruit children and destroy heterosexual marriages and proclaimed that AIDS was God's curse on homosexuals.

We would hear much more from the religious right in the years to come, and what amazed me was how consistently some prominent leaders used their platforms to persuade evangelicals to embrace a host of political positions that were neither religious nor right:

- Their response to the 9/11 attacks on America and the rise of global terrorism was Islamophobia and more tax dollars for weapons and soldiers to fight the ill-fated Iraq War of 2003–2011.
- Their support for Reagan-style, deregulated capitalism created the conditions that led to the Great Recession of 2007–2009.
- They opposed health care for poor and middle-class people, including 2010's Affordable Care Act, which they called Obamacare and condemned as socialism.

- Their approach to energy and the environment is simple: "Drill, baby, drill."
- Their approach to women's issues is to oppose policies that would benefit women and families: the Equal Rights Amendment, paid family leave, and equal pay for equal work.

Their approach to racial issues, not abortion, is what created the religious right. In 1954, the Supreme Court declared racially segregated school facilities unconstitutional. This decision made an activist out of Jerry Falwell, one of many leaders who created hundreds of "segregation academies." These private Christian schools refused to admit Black students. Falwell's Lynchburg Academy admitted its first Black student in 1979, the same year he founded the Moral Majority. Since then, the religious right's position on race has been to restrict immigration so America stays as white as possible.

Who Speaks for God?

Religious-right leaders have tried to disguise the ugliness of their political agenda by focusing on the abortion issue and convincing evangelicals to become single-issue voters betrothed to the Republican Grand Old Party (GOP). Using their powerful media outlets, leaders claimed their Republican-leaning policies were based on the principles of their faith and the teachings of God's Word. Scripture does not actually support their pet policies, but that has not stopped them from successfully converting a significant part of Christ's body into a passionately partisan political bloc.

That's wrong because Christians should be the ultimate swing voters, voting for Republicans when their values align with Christ's values, and voting for Democrats when their policies do so. Unfortunately, most evangelicals have not been taught to do that, but only to vote for the GOP.

To make matters worse, the nation's news media routinely referred to James Dobson, Jerry Falwell, and Pat Robertson as "evangelical leaders," suggesting that their views are representative of evangelical opinion in general, which we knew was not true. Evangelicalism is much more varied and diverse than the religious right.

The growing influence and destructive power of the religious right made me and many other evangelicals sad, frustrated, and angry. Our critique was not fundamentally political in nature, but spiritual and theological. We were convinced that the religious right's values and actions were not true to the Christian faith we followed, but they were instead twisting and hijacking the faith for raw political power.

I could see this same frustration and anger growing among young evangelicals around the country, many of whom have left the evangelical church after hearing too many sermons on culture wars and too few about Jesus.

I knew there were millions of people out there who felt the same way I did. Would there be some way to summon these frustrated believers to step up, let their voices be heard, and make their influence known?

In 2007, a group of us decided to find out by getting together and launching a new movement called Red Letter Christians, a term that signified our commitment to living by the words of Jesus, which in some Bibles are printed in red ink.

We felt an urgent need to do something because we believed that both our faith and our nation were in trouble, and if nothing were done, catastrophe loomed.

Our goal was to create a competing movement that would counteract harmful right-wing policies with constructive, nonpartisan policies that hewed closer to Jesus's values. But if you look around today, you can see that we fell short in our efforts.

The Gathering

Jim Wallis is a theologian, writer, and activist who founded Sojourners, which started as a community founded by students at Trinity Evangelical Divinity School and grew into a Washington-based social-justice organization that publishes the magazine of the same name. Jim's 2006 book, *God's Politics: Why the Right Gets It Wrong and the Left Doesn't Get It*, was a bestseller.

By 2007, the presidential campaign between John McCain and Obama was in full swing. At least in part to appease evangelicals who did not think McCain was conservative or godly enough, McCain chose Sarah Palin as his running mate.

Jim and I decided to organize a gathering of like-minded believers, and about thirty people showed up at Sojourners' offices, including the following, among others:

- Shane Claiborne, a former student of mine who would eventually become the group's leader;
- Ron Sider, a professor at Eastern Theological Seminary and author of numerous books, including the acclaimed *Rich Christians in an Age of Hunger*;
- Father Richard Rohr, a Catholic priest and Franciscan from New Mexico who teaches about the marriage of contemplation and action, and who helped us connect with other Catholics;
- Brian McLaren, a pastor, author, and leader in the "emerging church" movement;
- The Reverend Dr. Cheryl J. Sanders, a professor of Christian Ethics at the Howard University School of Divinity and senior pastor of the Third Street Church of God in Washington, DC;
- The Reverend Noel Castellanos, CEO and president of the Christian Community Development Association, a network

of hundreds of organizations that live and work in under-resourced neighborhoods;
- The Reverend Luis Cortes, the founder of Esperanza, America's largest evangelical network of Hispanic leaders, and a leader of Hispanic Clergy of Philadelphia;
- Jonathan Wilson-Hartgrove, another former student who is the assistant director for partnerships and fellowships at Yale University's Center for Public Theology and Public Policy.

Finding Our Mission

Group members agreed on a mission statement: "Staying true to the foundation of combining Jesus and justice, Red Letter Christians mobilizes individuals into *a movement of believers* who live out Jesus' counter-cultural teachings."[9]

We even had a "Red Letter Christian Pledge":

> I dedicate my life to Jesus, and commit to live as if Jesus meant the things he said in the "red letters" of Scripture.
>
> I will allow Jesus and his teaching to shape my decisions and priorities.
>
> I denounce belief-only Christianity and refuse to allow my faith to be a ticket into heaven and an excuse to ignore the suffering world around me.
>
> I will seek first the Kingdom of God—on earth as it is in heaven—and live in a way that moves the world towards God's dream, where the first are last and the last are first, where the poor are blessed and the peacemakers are the children of God, working towards a society where all are treated equally and resources shared equitably.
>
> I recognize that I will fall short in my attempts to follow Jesus, and I trust in God's grace and the community to catch me when I do.

> I know that I cannot do this alone, so I commit to share this journey with others who are walking in the way of Jesus. I will surround myself with people who remind me of Jesus, help me become more like him and hold me accountable for my actions and words.
>
> I will share Jesus with the world, with my words and with my deeds. Like Jesus, I will interrupt injustice, and stand up for the life and dignity of all. I will allow my life to point towards Christ, everywhere I go.[10]

When the news media asked us what we were up to, I said this: "The purpose of this gathering was not to create a religious left movement to challenge the religious right, but to jump-start a religious movement that will transcend partisan politics."

The Red and the Black

I guess you could say I have been a red-letter guy since I was ten years old. That's when my mother gave me my own Bible for Christmas, a leather-bound King James Version with the words of Jesus printed in red. This printing technique drew my attention to Jesus's words as I studied the New Testament.

As I grew in my faith, studied theology, and became a public figure, Jesus's teaching was at the core of my faith. I always believed that I should follow Jesus's message and method. Jesus's Sermon on the Mount, found in Matthew 5–7, became foundational for my personal devotion, my moral values, and my social activism.

Love your enemies. Blessed are the meek. Care for the poor. Turn the other cheek. The first shall be last. It does not get any more radical than this. Jesus's teaching turns our understanding of the world upside down. At least it did for me.

Jesus said he was bringing a bold new application of Old Testament teachings. Take a look at his method in this case, when he compares his message to the Ten Commandments (Exod. 20): "You have heard that it was said to the people long ago, 'You shall not murder, and anyone who murders will be subject to judgment.' But I tell you that anyone who is angry with a brother or sister will be subject to judgment" (Matt. 5:21–23).

Those of us who were Red Letter Christians grew concerned that many religious-right leaders, ministries, and broadcasters had forsaken both Jesus's message and his method. How so?

Message: Jesus often talked about caring for the poor and the outcast. He never once mentioned the two cardinal issues of the religious right: abortion and homosexuality. Why, we wondered, did conservative evangelicals elevate these two issues that Jesus never mentioned above the issues that Jesus actually stressed?

Method: Other than the times when he confronted legalistic religious leaders, Jesus's primary response to the sinners who surrounded him was love and compassion. But religious-right leaders showed anything but love to the people and groups they opposed.

We believed that Christians working in the public and political spheres should promote a more Christlike agenda: peace, building strong families, the elimination of poverty, the elimination of the death penalty, and more.

But soon after we publicly announced forming Red Letter Christians, there was a backlash in favor of the black letters of the Bible. *Christianity Today* critiqued us in an opinion piece by Stan Guthrie subtitled "Why I Am Not a Red-Letter Christian."[11] The piece critiqued our founding concept: "We evangelicals believe in the plenary, or full, inspiration of Scripture, don't we? Setting off Jesus' sayings this way seems to imply that they are more holy than what is printed in ordinary black ink."

I responded to the critique in a letter affirming the preeminence of Christ's teaching for Christians, and *Christianity Today* printed it in the next issue:

> While we, like you, have a very high view of the inspiration of Scripture and believe the Bible was divinely inspired, you are correct in accusing Red Letter Christians of giving the words of Jesus priority over all other passages of Scripture.
>
> I'm surprised you don't agree. After all, Stan, didn't Jesus himself make this same point in the Sermon on the Mount, when he said his teachings about marriage and divorce were to replace what Moses taught? Don't you think his red-letter words about loving our enemies and doing good to those who hurt us represent a higher morality than the "eye for an eye and a tooth for a tooth" kind of justice that we find in the Hebrew Testament? Is it really so hard to accept that, as God incarnate, Jesus set forth the highest law in the Bible, and therefore that law is more important than the Kosher dietary regulations we find in Leviticus and Deuteronomy?

Dynamic Duo

When a kid from rural eastern Tennessee named Shane Claiborne first showed up in my sociology class at Eastern University, he already had a passion for the poor. What the class gave him was a deeper appreciation for sociological understandings of how societies work, how institutions exert influence, and how social maladies are caused and can be corrected. He and I met for a year to discuss current events in light of Jesus's teachings.

During his junior year, he and some classmates got involved in advocacy for the city's homeless population. Since then, he has worked with Mother Teresa on the streets of Calcutta and with staff at Willow Creek, once one of the nation's most influential megachurches.

But decades later, Shane and his wife, Katie Jo, are back where they started, living and working in one of Philadelphia's roughest neighborhoods, where they lead the Simple Way, a Christian nonprofit that provides food and housing assistance to the poor.

Shane was a great student. He was thoughtful and committed to God. He has also turned out to be a darned good speaker and author. My favorite of Shane's books is *The Irresistible Revolution*, published in 2006.

Shane was a natural for Red Letter Christians, and in time he became a leading voice in the movement. The time had come for me to step into the background, get out of the way, and let Shane lead because I felt he was someone who could take our message to his generation. Shane was one who could talk to people about who Jesus is and how Jesus's values should be those Christians live by, both in private and public. Sure enough, Shane was soon a popular national speaker.

I wrote the movement's first book, *Red Letter Christians: A Citizen's Guide to Faith and Politics* (2008). That did well, so Shane and I worked together on a sequel: *Red Letter Revolution* (2012). The book's subtitle asks, *What If Jesus Really Meant What He Said?*

Shane and I became the key spokesmen for the Red Letter Christians, and after our book came out, we were often busy speaking at events and responding to inquiries from the news media who were trying to figure out what a progressive evangelical was.

Our book promotional tour took us to cities around the United States, as well as to a series of town halls across the United Kingdom, where our movement was warmly received.

Celebrations and Strategic Blunders

History shows that Red Letter Christians failed in its mission to gather a massive community of committed Jesus followers seeking an alternative to the "religious wrong" of the religious right. There are some clear reasons for our failures, but there are also many victories to celebrate.

One victory we achieved is changing the discussion. Today, more people realize that religious-right leaders are just part of the evangelical pie, and there are moderate and even left-leaning evangelicals too.

The media played a role in changing the discussion. Shane and I loved talking with reporters who were coming to see that religious-right leaders did not actually represent all evangelicals. We were covered by the *New York Times*, the *Washington Post*, and other major news outlets. I also enjoyed appearances on *The Colbert Report* with Stephen Colbert.

Because we were talking about the Red Letters, Shane and I often pointed journalists to passages in the Gospels in which Jesus spoke on the issues we were focusing on. Some of these interviews turned into intense personal discussions about God and faith.

Still, our many media impressions would never approach the messages churned out every day by hundreds of Christian radio stations from fire-breathing conservative political leaders. We actually did a weekly Red Letter Christians program for Trinity Broadcasting Network, but we should have had a daily radio show that could have reached a larger evangelical audience.

To our regret, we never created a robust organization that had its own board, office (we mostly used my office at Eastern), or fundraising campaign. Most of our income came from our leaders.

And at times, we wondered if our efforts to be nonpartisan actually prevented us from speaking out more forcefully against GOP policies we considered harmful.

We also failed to grasp the potent appeal of Christian nationalism. We saw plenty of conservatives claiming that America is a Christian nation, but we did not see the kind of blatant and idolatrous fusing of national and Christian identities that you see among many white evangelicals today.

Today there are 150 pro-Trump "prophets" claiming that God backs the former president. In the 1980s, Christian dominionism was a fringe doctrine. Today, more evangelicals embrace the view that Christian believers should rule over nonbelievers.

Many American evangelicals were totally unaware of our views, but Christians in Britain were much more responsive. Over the course of a few weeks, we spoke in overflowing town halls and met with church leaders, parachurch leaders, and members of Parliament who were trying to understand how their American brothers and sisters in Christ had replaced Jesus's message with a partisan political gospel.

Red Letter Christians had a particular appeal for an Irishman: Bono. The lead singer of U2, who had come to faith in a conservative Pentecostal group, wrote in his 2022 memoir, *Surrender*, about how our books and talks had helped him see that Jesus was concerned about justice, a topic the Bible mentions more than two thousand times.

Red vs. Black: The Debate Continues

Two decades after *Christianity Today* critiqued Red Letter Christians, the magazine complimented us, at least somewhat, thanks to a column by editor in chief Russell Moore.[12] He admits, "There was a time when I was really worried about 'red-letter Christianity,'" but now he sees a new worry. "Increasingly, I'm seeing its mirror image, a kind of 'black-letter Christianity' which is just as perilous." Moore explains:

> Over the past several years, we've had some evangelical leaders, and the politicians they support, ridicule the "weakness" implied in "Turn the other cheek." If that were just the Bizarro world of cable television news, I would perhaps dismiss it. But several pastors have told me about how when they cited, parenthetically, "Turn the other cheek" or "Love your enemies," they had someone ask afterward where they were getting their "liberal" ideas.

> Another told me that after preaching on the Sermon on the Mount, a congregant told him, "We've tried the 'Turn the other cheek' stuff, it doesn't work; it's time now to fight."

I do not expect Russell Moore to join Red Letter Christians anytime soon, but I appreciate him for understanding what we're trying to do. As he concludes:

> The Bible is black and white and red all over.
>
> But the red-letter Christians are right to remind us that when we see Jesus, we have seen the Father (John 14:9). . . .
>
> The whole plot line of the Bible holds together in one person—the living Jesus of Nazareth. Less clear passages are interpreted by those that are clearer—and the clearest revelation of all is this person who said to us, "Come follow me."
>
> In other words: Jesus loves me, this I know, for the Bible tells me so.

PART 5

THE END OF THE ROAD

CHAPTER 26

A TIME OF LOSS

On the morning of June 8, 2015, I released a public statement clarifying that I now believed that same-sex couples should be given the same privileges and blessings that heterosexual couples enjoy within the intimacy of marriage.

Less than three weeks later, the United States Supreme Court announced its ruling in *Obergefell v. Hodges*, concluding: "The fundamental right to marry is guaranteed to same-sex couples by both the Due Process Clause and the Equal Protection Clause of the Fourteenth Amendment of the Constitution."

Conservative Christians condemned the Court's decision, and many condemned me, too, as it seemed that just about every major Christian denomination was on the verge of schism over this controversial issue.

June 2015 began a five-year period of loss that saw me reduce my teaching load at Eastern University and suffer a debilitating stroke that would leave me partially disabled, effectively ending my public ministry.

A Sunday Surprise

For years, Peggy and I traveled the country with a tag-team presentation designed to help congregations navigate the bitter divisions over the role of homosexual people in Christ's church. During her part of the presentation, Peggy would tell her story of ministering to LGBTQ people who felt persecuted by the church. Peggy would then endorse the full inclusion of LGBTQ people in the church and argue in favor of same-sex marriage.

During my part of the presentation, I explained my journey and my theology of homosexuality. Like Peggy, I affirmed that churches should be open and welcoming to everyone. But unlike Peggy, I always concluded my portion of our talks by reaffirming my view that God had designed marriage for men and women, not same-sex couples. Still, I always reminded people that while I (then) felt same-sex marriage was sinful, God commands me to show the same love to all people, regardless of their sexual orientation.

Then, during the final part of our presentation, Peggy and I would talk about how we still loved and respected each other, despite our differences over this hot-button topic. In some cases, we would talk about the tensions our division over this issue had caused in our marriage, but how we remained a couple, united in purpose. Our goal was to help church members coexist amid disagreements on the topic, rather than breaking fellowship and finding churches that were more amenable to their views.

This was our established routine, and we took it on the road. But on Sunday, June 21, 2015, I flipped the script. Peggy and I were speaking at a Methodist church in West Virginia. After Peggy gave her talk, I rose for my part of the presentation. Standing in the church's pulpit, I surprised myself and shocked Peggy by announcing the change that had happened in my mind and heart the previous night in our hotel room.

"For years, I have opposed gay marriage on biblical and theological grounds, but upon further reflection I feel I can no longer maintain this position," I said.

Peggy was overjoyed, but I did not sleep that night, worrying about how my new views could cause the ministries I supported to back away from me.

Evolving Theology on Sexuality

I had not undergone a dramatic conversion, but my views had evolved. What pushed me over the edge was my belief that God wanted his gay and lesbian children to experience the same joy and intimacy in marriage that I had experienced with Peggy. Marriage had been a beautiful blessing for me, and it had helped me grow emotionally and spiritually in so many ways. How could I deny that provision to gays and lesbians?

I kept coming back to two scientific truths about homosexuality I had learned over the years:

1. *Nobody knows what causes homosexual orientation.* Many evangelicals continue to maintain that homosexuality is a choice, but the evidence does not support that. I challenged them by turning the table. "If sexual orientation is a choice, would you mind telling me when you chose to be a heterosexual?"

Other evangelicals offer a Neo-Freudian take, claiming that boys become gay when they grow up with a strong mother and weak father. This blames parents for messing up and raising gay kids. But if this were the case, I should have been gay. The evidence does not support that view, either.

2. *Once a homosexual orientation is established, it's close to impossible to change it.* I'm not saying it's impossible, because I have seen situations in which people who previously considered themselves to be gay later identify as straight. But this does not happen often, and Christians who insist that gay kids change can cause horrible emotional suffering, leading some to commit suicide.

Making My Case

A reporter with the United Methodist News Service was sitting in the back of the church that day. She informed me that she planned to write an article about my change of heart. If it had not been for her writing that article, I probably never would have released my June 26 statements supporting same-sex marriage.

Bart pressed me to get in front of the story by releasing my statement, so I would have the ability to describe my position clearly.

"Are you going to let somebody else define your position?" he repeatedly asked me.

Bart wanted me to explain myself, not have someone else explain my views, so he and I worked on my statement, taking it through numerous drafts before finally releasing it at around 9 a.m. June 26.

I thought that would be the end of the matter. Boy, was I wrong.

I was aware that the Court was considering the *Obergefell* case, but I had no idea what the justices would conclude or when.

Within an hour, my phone was ringing, first with congratulatory calls from supportive friends, followed by condemning calls from conservative Christian critics. Then came reporters wanting to do stories on my announcement. One reporter predicted that my change of heart would be a tipping point for the evangelical movement. Fat chance!

Over the next few days, stories about my support for same-sex marriage would run in the secular and Christian press. Almost immediately, evangelical churches that had contracted with me to speak canceled these engagements. I also lost my opportunity to speak on behalf of Compassion International and World Vision, two ministries that depended on conservative Christian donors for significant portions of their income.

I was sad about losing these speaking engagements, not only because I loved speaking to groups, but also because I could raise significant funds for these two ministries, as well as EAPE, the ministry I had founded. But there was nothing I could do. I could not go back and erase my words or say I'm sorry.

The reporter from United Methodist News Service never

published her article. She felt it would bring too much condemnation to the West Virginia church where we spoke.

Other Christian leaders faced similar challenges over this complicated issue. Eugene Peterson is the author of many books, including *The Message* version of the Bible. Two years after I released my statement, Peterson told a reporter that he had become more supportive of same-sex marriage. The blowback was so significant that he quickly recanted.[13]

In early 2023, as I was working on this chapter, the pope weighed in, saying that while the church teaches that homosexuality is a sin, it should not be a crime. Churches and Christian institutions can decide how they will address these issues, but I worry about forcing people out of our churches. And I do not believe conservative Christians should use their political power and influence to turn their list of sins into laws that criminalize and punish fellow Americans because of who they love.

Lightening My Load at Eastern

Even though there were many churches that would not invite me to speak because of my position on same-sex marriage, many other churches and ministries continued to invite me. That kept me on the road more than one hundred days a year, but my busy schedule was becoming a concern for my family.

I was becoming physically and mentally worn down. I was moving so quickly that I no longer had the time to read and to think—two activities that were essential to my role as a public theologian, speaker, teacher, and author. I could see the results when I spoke or preached. My talks became repetitious and thin on new content.

Bart took the initiative, and without me knowing anything about it he approached David Black, the president of Eastern (and a good family friend), pleading with David to reduce my teaching load.

"I need you to help me save my father's life," Bart told President Black.

Soon, my teaching load was lessened. But I continued teaching, and students continued to sign up for Eastern's Campolo Center for Ministry.

Some people have claimed that Eastern reduced my load in response to my new position supporting same-sex marriage. But that was not the case. It is true, however, that my position led some students and donors to go elsewhere.

In fact, in 2022 Eastern announced that it will now hire LGBTQ employees, a stance that put a hold on its membership in the Council for Christian Colleges and Universities, which says that member colleges' hiring policies should reflect "the historic Christian view of marriage."

Bart's efforts to slow me down were loving and well-intentioned, but they failed to take me off the road. My aging body would take care of that.

Hobbled in Honolulu

Hawaiian Islands Ministries supports and encourages pastors, a mission that is near and dear to my heart, as it is to Dan Chun, who founded the ministry in 1983. Peggy and I served on the ministry's board, and I was a frequent speaker at their conferences, which are offered to many pastors at no charge.

I delivered my final plenary session in Honolulu on Thursday morning, April 4, 2002. My bags were packed because I needed to catch a flight to Dallas, and from there to Boston, where I would connect with Peggy on Saturday for an important series of talks at Harvard University starting on Monday. I would be the Easter Missioner at Harvard's Memorial Church. During the week, I would also give talks to some classes and student groups. I was excited to bring messages about Jesus to this diverse and theologically liberal institution.

But something unusual happened as I made my way from the Honolulu hotel hosting the pastors conference to the taxi that was waiting for me. I stumbled and temporarily lost my balance, not because I tripped on a gap in the sidewalk, but because something inside me was not working right.

I made it to Dallas, and then to Boston, but my body still was not quite right. I normally used my time on flights to write thank-you notes to donors and friends, but this time my hand was shaking, and my handwriting was messy and nearly illegible.

By the time Peggy and I reached our hotel in Boston, I felt dizzy enough that I asked her to have the hotel call an ambulance, which whisked me to Mount Auburn Hospital in Cambridge. I was taken care of by a young doctor who was a graduate of Wheaton College and had heard me speak in chapel services there.

He told me there was no way he was going to permit me to leave the hospital for my events at Harvard. I told him there was no way he was going to stop me, and I knew he lacked legal means to restrain me.

In the end, we made a deal. I would leave the hospital, and he would sit in the front row at the chapel service the next morning to be on hand in case of a further emergency. Meanwhile, after I concluded each talk, I would return to the hospital for further tests.

A "Miracle" at Harvard

It was a beautiful week of meetings and chapel services. At each service, I offered an invitation for people to step forward and accept Christ as their Savior, and each time a few did. But things did not always go smoothly.

At one service, I asked the congregation to join me in singing the famous Billy Graham crusade invitation song, "Just as I Am." It soon became clear that neither the chapel's classically trained organist, nor its choir, nor the people in the pews were familiar with the song. So, the Reverend Peter J. Gomes, Harvard's evangelical chaplain, rose to his feet to lead the singing, playing the role of Graham's musical sidekick, Cliff Barrows. That evening, after spirited singing, a larger-than-normal group of people knelt at the altar.

Gomes later told me it was a "miracle" that the student newspaper, the *Harvard Crimson*, had covered each of my chapel talks because he had been unable to attract editors' attention with other chapel events.

"If I could have staged a live crucifixion at the chapel, I wouldn't have generated the coverage that you've been getting each night," he told me.

My stroke effects were minor, and as I improved, I continued my busy speaking schedule. Two weeks after speaking at Harvard, I was back in Honolulu speaking at the historic Central Union Church when a woman came to speak with me.

"I'm not a Christian," she told me, "but I wanted to come here today to hear you because the pagan daughter I sent off to Harvard became a Christian during the time you were there."

It looked as if life would go on as normal, and it did for the next eighteen years. I would not be so lucky the next time.

My Brain Attack

It hit me on June 20, 2020. I had spent part of the morning in the gym at Beaumont at Bryn Mawr, the retirement community Peggy and I moved into in 2006, four years after my incident in Hawaii. I love living here because the grass is cut and the snow is shoveled without my involvement.

I came back from the gym to shower and shave, but as I was shaving, something overtook me. I keeled over and landed in a heap on the floor. It was not a heart attack, but a brain attack—a massive stroke. I called out to Peggy, who rallied staff and found someone to take me to the hospital.

I yearned for a quick recovery so I could get back out on the road again. But that was not to be. Doctors told Peggy and Lisa that I was partially paralyzed, and after many long, hard months of rehabilitative therapy, it became clear that my condition was likely permanent. I would need to accept my new limitations, and everybody else in the family would have to help me out.

Doctors tried to tell me this, too, but it never registered with me. This was not something I was ready to accept, and I vented my frustration to doctors, Peggy, Lisa, and anyone else who insisted on telling me the truth.

"Even if I'm stuck in a wheelchair, I can still get out there and speak," I claimed. But my chorus of naysayers repeatedly let me know that would happen when pigs flew.

In time, I found that I was able to walk, somewhat, with a special walker that the medical staff at Beaumont gave me. I was convinced that, with enough physical therapy, I would recover and walk again. I needed nursing staff to accompany me as I wheeled down the hallway with my walker so that I would not fall and hurt myself, but there were some days when they were unable to devote all their time to helping me. I was so angry and frustrated.

I knew things were serious when my assistant began calling churches that had booked me so he could cancel my events. Bart also helped get the word out to friends and associates.

I should have been appreciative, but I was not. I felt that everyone was taking control of my life and not allowing me to make any decisions. I know it was for the best, but I still cannot help feeling somewhat ticked off about it all.

There are still days when I harbor the belief that, with proper help, I can get around with my walker, grow stronger, and walk again. But then reality sets in once again, and I realize that my public ministry, which defined me for decades, is irrefutably over. These are very sad moments for me.

Lisa tells me that I ought to be grateful the stroke did not affect my brain.

"You still can think, and you can still write," she told me. "Why don't you get on with what you can do instead of being depressed about what you can't do?"

This advice makes sense, but I cannot stop thinking about all the things I used to do before but cannot even attempt today.

Who Am I Now?

As the truth of my circumstances began to sink in, I was overcome by a profound identity crisis. For decades, my preaching and teaching and speaking had become the things around which I organized my identity.

Now I stayed awake at nights asking myself, "If I'm not a pastor anymore, and if I'm not a university professor anymore, and if I'm not a speaker on the evangelical speaking circuit, who am I?"

To make matters worse, after the stroke Peggy and I had to move out of the apartment we shared at Beaumont because I now needed a room with more nursing care. The worst part of the move was the thinning of my library. I used to know where all my key books were and would ask Peggy to retrieve a book based on its color or location on my bookshelves. Bart and Lisa took charge of the project, deciding which books would come with me to my smaller room and which books would wind up in stacks of cardboard boxes. I still miss so many of those precious books.

In addition to my identity crisis and diminished library, I was facing new questions that took me into a crisis of faith. I wondered where God was, why he had allowed this to happen to me, and how he could let something like this happen to one of his devoted servants.

"I've been one of your faithful soldiers," I pleaded to God. "Why are you allowing me to be shut down like this?"

For decades, my theology was something I worked out in the context of interacting with young people and preparing lectures and sermons. I was constantly asking, "What is most relevant to my audience? What words and images can I use to express the position I'm proposing?" This thinking through of my positions and figuring out the best words to describe my theology was very crucial.

Now I was robbed of these steps. I was deprived of the social give-and-take that led me to reflect on my theology, as well as the opportunity to articulate it to others. I had not only lost any opportunities to speak, but I had also lost the very things that gave me a sense of who I was and what my life was about. This has been a traumatic experience, and I have not recovered from it.

Over the years I had become friends with Elton Trueblood, a beloved Quaker author, theologian, and speaker. I wrote an article about him in *Christianity Today*, "The Quiet Revolutionary," which described how aging had affected this ninety-one-year-old man of God: "His gait has slowed, his age shows in the sags and lines of his face, and his voice wavers, but he still stands tall and shakes hands with a firm grip."[14]

As I was dealing with my identity crisis, I went to see Elton again, now nearing one hundred, at the nearby retirement community where he lived. He told me he had experienced the same problem. For decades, he developed his theology in conjunction with his speaking, and since his speaking had ended, his theological reflection had declined somewhat. I wonder how many other speakers, writers, and leaders have dealt with this kind of dislocation.

I spent so many years speaking to young people and focusing on their concerns that I never spent much time developing a theology of aging or preparing myself for the inevitable losses that aging brings with it. I never gave much thought to what older people should do with their lives, and now I regret that oversight.

I am still struggling to adapt to my new reality, which is why, on some nights, I lie in bed and, instead of counting sheep, I ask myself one very simple question: "Who am I?"

CHAPTER 27

SUNDAYS AT BEAUMONT

Before long, I realized something significant was missing. There was no Sunday church service in the Beaumont nursing facility, which struck me as odd because many of us here are preparing to meet our Maker at any moment. Wouldn't it be nice if we could commune with and worship him while we're still alive?

In 2020, I felt called to reprise my role as Pastor Tony so I could lead a weekly chapel service at 2 p.m. on Sundays.

The contrast with my previous speaking engagements could not be more dramatic. In the past I spoke to tens of thousands of people at a time at huge outdoor Christian festivals, or to a few thousand church youth workers in big convention halls. Now, I preach to ten to fourteen people who gather in a small, fluorescent-lit recreation room.

Back in my heady public-speaking days, energetic hosts would introduce me to big crowds that were warmed up and enthusiastic to hear me. Now I preach to low-energy seniors who roll into our meeting in wheelchairs, just as I do, and who struggle to stay awake—the consequence of competing with afternoon nap time. Peggy contributes by reading each week's Scripture passage.

In the past I often spoke after groups enjoyed times of rousing singing, typically high-energy praise choruses. Now, few of us can sing all that well. Some Sundays, I simply read a few verses of one of my favorites from a hymnal:

> My hope is built on nothing less
> Than Jesus' blood and righteousness
> I dare not trust the sweetest frame
> But wholly lean on Jesus' name.

I have found that some of the classic hymns read like poetry:

> Once to every man and nation
> Comes the moment to decide,
> In the strife of truth with falsehood,
> For the good or evil side;
> Some great cause, God's new Messiah,
> Offering each the bloom or blight,
> And the choice goes by forever
> Twixt that darkness and that light.

Everyone is happier on those Sundays when Barbara feels well enough to join us. Once an accomplished singer and church soloist, she still loves singing her favorite hymn for us when we request it:

> I walked today where Jesus walked,
> In days of long ago.
> I wandered down each path He knew,
> With reverent step and slow.
> Those little lanes, they have not changed,
> A sweet peace fills the air.
> I walked today where Jesus walked,
> And felt His presence there.

Some Sundays, Barbara surprises us with songs that do not

appear in any hymnal, like "I Feel Pretty" from the musical *West Side Story*:

> I feel pretty
> Oh, so pretty
> I feel pretty, and witty, and bright

"Thank you, Barbara," I said after she finished singing. "That song is perfect for us because that's exactly how God sees us right now. We may be old and weak, but we are beautiful in his sight."

Sermons for Seniors

The topics I address with my aged congregation are different from those I addressed when I used Scripture and sociology to focus on the concerns of young people and the pressing social issues of the day.

Death is a recurring theme. Members of my little flock realize their days are numbered, and they want to talk about what awaits them. Christians often hear sermons about life after death, but for most of us death remains a remote abstraction. For those of us in Beaumont's medical wing, however, death is a daily existential reality. Each one of us knows the truth. "I could be the next to go." This realization is sobering, and it focuses our minds and hearts on God.

One Sunday, I based my sermon on the shortest verse in the Bible: "Jesus wept" (John 11:35). Why was Jesus sorrowful? Because of the death of his friend Lazarus. It's a sad story for an audience well acquainted with grief. But then in the next moment: a miracle. Jesus raises Lazarus from the dead in a preview of the joy of new life Christians will experience in heaven.

"Jesus brought Lazarus back to life," I tell my little flock, "and that's what he's going to do for all of us. We will be with him for all eternity if we trust in him for our salvation."

Other sermons explore Jesus's promise to his worried disciples that he would prepare a place for his followers in heaven: "Do not let your hearts be troubled. You believe in God; believe also in me. My Father's house has many rooms; if that were not so, would I have told you that I am going there to prepare a place for you? And if I go and prepare a place for you, I will come back and take you to be with me so that you also may be where I am. You know the way to the place where I am going" (John 14:1–4).

Invitations and Challenges

For as long as I have given sermons and talks, I have nearly always concluded with an invitation and a challenge because I want people to act on what they have heard. My Beaumont flock has forced me to adapt my old approach.

In years past, I invited people to walk down the aisle, kneel at the altar, and give their lives to Christ. But members of my current flock can neither walk nor kneel, and our little recreation room has no aisle. So, I simply ask everyone to give their lives to Christ, whether for the very first time or the latest time.

"When you accept Jesus in your heart, your sins are forgiven, forgotten, and buried in the deepest sea, to be remembered no more," I tell them.

That promise is welcome news to older people whose minds are flooded with memories of could haves and should haves and are wracked with guilt over past sins. "Ask Jesus to forgive you, and accept his forgiveness," I beg them.

It's the challenge part of my sermon that I have changed the most in adapting to the needs of my current flock. Back in my go-go days of public speaking, I would challenge my audiences of mostly young people to devote their lives to Christian service, whether in leading a church, serving as a missionary, or meeting the needs of the poor.

"Jesus wants you to become agents of Christ so you can go to work in this world, changing things from what they are to what God wants them to be," I cried out.

Since my Beaumont brothers and sisters do not have decades of life they can devote to Christ's service, I tailor my challenges to them, often challenging myself more than I move them.

Picture Jesus among Us

The sheep of my flock are not about to serve as missionaries in Tanzania, but they can be agents of Christ here at Beaumont, as I told them in a recent sermon, "What Would Jesus Do?"

"So, what would Jesus do if he were here with us today, sitting in a wheelchair just like you and me? What kind of ministry could Christ have here at Beaumont?"

The notion surprises some of them, so I give them a moment to ponder it before offering my answer.

"I think he would love the nurses and attendants who take care of us every day, who get us out of bed, who take us to the toilet, who clean us and dress us up. He wouldn't grumble at them, like I sometimes do when I get cranky and get mad at God for allowing me to suffer a stroke and lose my career.

"He wouldn't ignore them, or overlook them, or look down on them, like we sometimes do. Instead, he would love them, cherish them, thank them, and praise them for treating us with the dignity, respect, and love they show us day after day."

I looked at each one of the men and women listening to me as I emphasized the sermon's point: no matter who you are, or where you are, or how old and infirm you are, there's always something you can do for Christ, even if it's something as simple as blessing the people who care for you.

I closed that Sunday with a simple prayer:

"Lord, I pray that thy will be done right here at Beaumont, as it is in heaven. Lord, help me to be your instrument for making this an outpost of the kingdom of God. Let the workers and guests who come into our section see something incredibly lovely here. In Jesus's name. Amen."

Forgive

I have given my flock a number of sermons from Jesus's Sermon on the Mount (Matt. 5–7), including a few about these two powerful charges: "And forgive us our debts, as we also have forgiven our debtors" (Matt. 6:12).

Some seniors carry extensive and heavy psychological baggage. Some feel anger at those who have wronged them or neglected them. One woman struggles to forgive her husband for the broken trust that came from his affair many years ago.

Some feel tremendous guilt over wrongs they committed against others. For them, forgiving themselves may be the hardest thing.

I understand their struggles. Even though I'm largely content and at peace with God and my life, difficult and jagged memories frequently nag at me as I reflect on nearly nine decades' worth of missed opportunities and what-ifs.

Why didn't I love Peggy more by giving her more of myself? And how could I have allowed myself to hurt her—and others—so much for so long with my callous views about LGBTQ people?

Why wasn't I a better father to Lisa and Bart?

Why couldn't I be a better pastor at the churches I served? Why did I do so many topical sermons on current topics, instead of guiding people through books of the Bible? Why didn't I have more patience and love for the people who opposed my efforts to racially integrate their communities? Why did I try to do so much myself, instead of training up young Timothys and delegating more ministry responsibilities to them? Why didn't I organize weekly healing services so deacons and I could pray with people who desperately needed a healing touch in their lives?

"Look," I tell them. "I understand what it means to be nagged by doubts and guilt and regret about life. I understand what it means to be angry at others who have done me wrong. But I refuse to let guilt and resentment steal my joy and peace in my final years. Don't let the devil whisper in your ear and fill your head with negative self-talk."

I quote a few more lines from Jesus's Sermon on the Mount: "And lead us not into temptation, but deliver us from the evil one" (Matt. 6:13).

Have an Attitude of Gratitude

"How many times have you prayed, 'Lord, give us today our daily bread'?" I ask them, letting the question hang in the air for a minute.

"Millions of times," one woman said.

"Me too. But how many times have we thanked God for delivering on that request? Our lunch today was pretty good, wasn't it? In fact, all of us here enjoy pretty good food at every meal, don't we? Let's remember to be grateful to God for that, while remembering to pray and care for those who don't enjoy such bounty."

Seniors can be troubled by many things, but gratitude has a way of changing our perspective and helping us see the many good gifts we enjoy.

Make the Most of Your Time

"There are many things we are no longer capable of doing, but there are many things we can do now that we couldn't—or wouldn't—do before," I tell them.

"Prayer is one of those things we can do even amid our infirmities, and many of us can be more devoted to prayer now. Instead of spending all day watching TV, devote some of your time to praying for us, for staff, for loved ones, and for the world," I preach.

"Those aren't the only ways we can love God and love our neighbor today. You can make phone calls to people who may be shut in or sick. You can write notes of encouragement to people and send them greeting cards on their birthdays and other occasions."

My words often lead me to call a friend I have not spoken to in a while.

"Think about what you're going to do with the money you leave behind," I challenge them. "Make sure you use it for maximum good for others and the kingdom of God. And don't give to some crackpot televangelist for a new jet."

Q&A

After each sermon, I check to see if anybody has any questions or items they want to discuss. They often do.

"Do we go to heaven right away, or does it take time?" one woman asked.

If I was talking to a college group about this, I would answer by referencing Einstein's theories about time, space, and eternity, but these are not college students interested in scientific theories, so I answer her directly.

"No waiting," I told her. "I believe Scripture teaches that at the moment of death the person who is in Christ is immediately present with the Lord. God is eternal, and as it says in Psalm 90: 'A thousand years in your sight are like a day that has just gone by.'"

I added: "With God, the time between your death and the moment you stand in the presence of God is compressed into one eternal now. It will seem as if you get there in an instant."

"Will my husband and loved ones be there waiting for me?" asked another woman. I mentioned Paul's teaching about our resurrected bodies: "For the trumpet will sound, the dead will be raised imperishable, and we will be changed. For the perishable must clothe itself with the imperishable, and the mortal with immortality" (1 Cor. 15:52–53).

Our little flock's members struggle daily with a range of physical ailments and limitations, so the promise of a new body is exciting.

"Yes," I told her. "Your loved ones will be there, and you will be able to recognize them in your resurrected body, and they will recognize you. All of our ailments and physical disabilities, like being unable to walk, or blindness, will be taken care of. We will be whole again."

One occasional member of our flock was a Jewish man who had retired from teaching physics at the University of Pennsylvania. He was intrigued by Jesus's description of a house in heaven with many rooms.

"My rabbi never promises eternal life," he told me one Friday afternoon as we talked. He would later ask me to deliver his memorial sermon.

I have been thinking more about heaven myself. I cannot wait to see it, to be with my mother and father and sisters again, and to inhabit my new, resurrected body.

I also tell my congregation that I believe God will have something meaningful for each one of us to do in heaven. I would like to work with some kind of heavenly Young Life group. But others may find their heavenly purpose in building deeper relationships with loved ones, singing beautiful songs of praise to God, raising beautiful gardens, or contemplating the Divine.

Good and Faithful Servant

I'm not bluffing them. Overall, I'm content, at peace, and ready to meet my Maker. While I cannot say I have no anxieties, I'm less anxious than ever as I sense the grace of God more and more.

Death does not worry or threaten me. As the Orthodox Christian liturgy says, I trust in the grace of God and believe that, on the cross, Jesus became everything that was ugly about who I am, and I became wonderfully clothed in his righteousness. I will walk before the judgment seat boldly because I know that my sins have all been forgiven, forgotten, buried, and remembered no more.

I hope that when I stand before God, he will use the words from Jesus's parable about three servants (Matt. 25:14–30) and declare me a "good and faithful servant." I feel as if I tried to do what God wanted me to do, and I gave it everything I had.

Nearly a half century ago, when I was only about forty, I got together with two other Christian leaders to talk about what we wanted to do with the rest of our lives. I remember telling them that I wanted to look back and say that there were one hundred young people who made commitments to go into ministry of one kind or another through my speaking ministry.

Looking back on that now, I'm grateful that God gave me this calling and helped me fulfill it, and I look forward to hearing all about everything they did.

Sometimes I lie in bed wondering what will happen to Peggy when I'm gone. What will happen to Eastern University? What about America? What about the evangelical church? Will it end its decades-long marriage to the GOP and return to its first love, Jesus?

All I can do now is pray and hope.

Among my prayers of thanks, I regularly remember the Bible Buzzards, the group of on-fire Christians I started hanging out with in the eighth grade. They introduced me to Christ and the power of the Holy Spirit in ways I might never have experienced had I simply continued to attend church with my parents.

The Buzzards showed me what it meant to be passionately committed to Christ and his service. That passion still fires me seventy-five years later.

My earthly pilgrimage has been an amazing journey, and when my life ends, I will be ready to abandon this worn-out body and overtaxed mind and rest in the presence of God for all eternity.

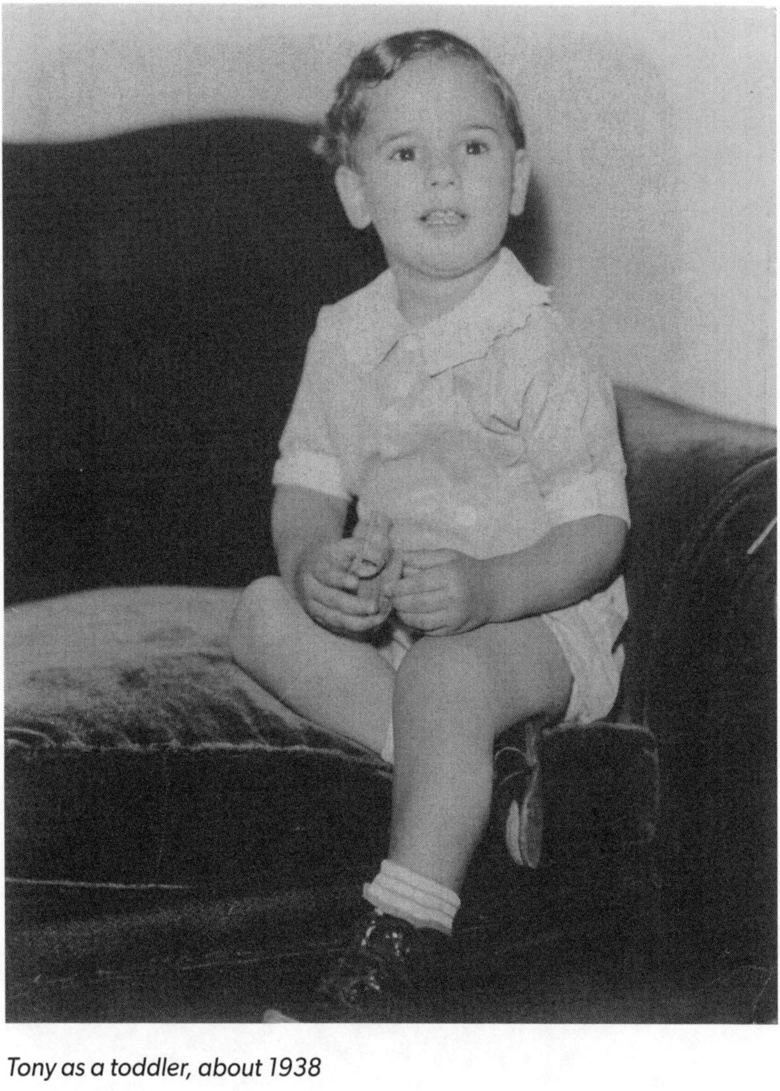

Tony as a toddler, about 1938

Tony as a little drummer boy, about 1942

Father and son in their Sunday best, West Philadelphia

Potrait of a young scholar

Peggy Davidson as a college student

Tony as a college student

Albert Einstein with the 1949 Greater Philadelphia Science Fair award winners (Tony in back row, sixth from right)

Tony and his parents, celebrating a happy occasion

Tony and Peggy's first home together, a farmer's tenant house in Chesterfield, New Jersey, 1958

Peggy and Tony with Bart and Lisa, Christmas 1963

Lisa and Bart, Christmas 1968

Bart with race car driver Roger McCluskey, summer 1970

The Campolo family, Christmas 1973

All smiles on the EAPE mission field

Tony visiting with children in Haiti

Tony with EAPE volunteers, on the steps of the Philadelphia Art Museum

On the campaign trail in Overbrook—Campolo for Congress '76!

Peggy and Tony at a Congressional campaign fundraiser, 1976

Tony at the podium, at a Penn Marva Milk Producers event, 1982

Tony at the US Capitol Building, as a candidate for Congress in 1976

I'd like you to meet my son, Bart

He is an experienced speaker who shares my concerns for youth, the Third World, and the inner city. Bart has travelled with me to Haiti and the Dominican Republic, and has served as youth pastor at a church here in Pennsylvania. Recently he worked as on-site director of our summer program in the Bartram Village section of Philadelphia.

Bart has a passion for the needs of the poor. He is an outstanding communicator.

Tony Campolo

Bart Campolo, c/o Dr. Anthony Campolo, Eastern College, St. Davids, PA 19087

Introducing . . . Bart!

Tony in his element, traveling abroad and looking around the next corner

ACKNOWLEDGMENTS

I would like to thank the following people.

My wife, Peggy, who has long inspired my writing, and who has always been more convinced that I could produce helpful books than I've ever been. I thank Peggy for her lifelong patience and input, especially for her interest in this project, and for making sure that I was up and ready for phone conferences with my coauthor.

I will be eternally grateful to my daughter, Lisa Goodheart, and my son, Bart Campolo, for their willingness to scrutinize the manuscript for errors, distortions, and exaggerations, in the interest of helping me try to get things right.

I thank Eastern University for its support for this project and for its half-century influence on my life and faith. I could not have achieved what I did in my life without the good people of Eastern.

Robert Gauthier, the executive director of the Campolo Center for Ministry at Eastern University, has kept the center alive and growing beyond anyone's expectations. Since my stroke, this man has carried me, both figuratively and physically.

My heartfelt gratitude goes to the staff and the health care team at Beaumont in Bryn Mawr, the retirement community where Peggy and I have lived for nearly two decades. Day in and day out, they do the hard work of keeping me fed, clothed, clean, safe, and comfortable. They treat me with kindness, respect, and good humor, and I am more grateful for their faithful support than I could ever express. I will not attempt to list them all by name, lest I leave anyone out through an oversight, but they know who they are, and I want them each to know how deeply I appreciate them.

I'm especially appreciative of Steve Rabey, who faithfully interviewed me for this book week after week and year after year, challenging me to articulate the events of my life in theological terms in ways I would not have done otherwise. Working with Steve was a joy.

Veteran editor and writer Douglas LeBlanc incorporated hundreds of edits, updates, and revisions, helping to make this book ready for your reading pleasure.

And finally, thanks to editor Andrew Knapp and the entire team at Eerdmans for helping prepare this volume for publication. Eerdmans' publication of this book, which I know will be my last, is greatly appreciated.

NOTES

1. Elizabeth Eisenstadt Evans, "Eastern University Has Served as the Evangelical Left's Laboratory," *The Christian Century*, May 5, 2021, https://tinyurl.com/8xyf5ecx.

2. Jan Willem Vink, "Steve Camp: Feeding the Sheep, Not Entertaining the Goats," *Cross Rhythms*, February 1, 1992, https://tinyurl.com/3b3p5xvh.

3. Ted Olsen, "The Positive Prophet," *Christianity Today*, January 1, 2003, https://tinyurl.com/yckhj4xp.

4. Randy Frame, "Evangelical Leaders Judge Tony Campolo's Theology," *Christianity Today*, December 13, 1985, https://tinyurl.com/yy53cfkb.

5. Frame, "Evangelical Leaders Judge Tony Campolo's Theology."

6. See "Corrections," *New York Times*, September 17, 1998, https://tinyurl.com/4wc24kp7.

7. Jonathan Merritt, "Tony Campolo's Surprise Reaction When His Son Came Out as a Humanist," Religion News Service, October 6, 2014, https://tinyurl.com/3h7rbae2.

8. Mark Oppenheimer, "The Evangelical Scion Who Stopped Believing," *New York Times*, December 29, 2016, https://tinyurl.com/bdz9fr7w.

9. See "Our Mission & Our Story," Red Letter Christians, accessed April 17, 2024, https://tinyurl.com/jwb9k388.

10. See "Join the Movement," Red Letter Christians, accessed April 17, 2024, https://tinyurl.com/mtjztey7.

11. Stan Guthrie, "When Red Is Blue," *Christianity Today*, October 11, 2007, https://tinyurl.com/ydt9ytdw. My response follows Guthrie's column at the same URL.

12. Russell Moore, "Revenge of the Black-Letter Christians," *Christianity Today*, March 10, 2022, https://tinyurl.com/ewp42xbp.

13. Kate Shellnutt, "Actually, Eugene Peterson Does Not Support Same-Sex Marriage," *Christianity Today*, July 13, 2017, https://tinyurl.com/mr43ha5h.

14. Tony Campolo, "The Quiet Revolutionary," *Christianity Today*, February 11, 1991, https://tinyurl.com/2cv77pap.

BOOKS BY TONY CAMPOLO

A Denomination Looks at Itself (Judson Press, 1971)
The Success Fantasy (Victory Press, 1980)
The Power Delusion (Victory Press, 1983)
A Reasonable Faith (Thomas Nelson, 1983)
Ideas for Social Action: A Handbook on Mission and Service for Christian Young People (Zondervan, 1984)
You Can Make a Difference (Word Publishing, 1984)
It's Friday, but Sunday's Comin' (Word Publishing, 1984)
Partly Right: Christianity Responds to Its Critics (Word Publishing, 1985)
Seven Deadly Sins (Victor Books, 1987)
Who Switched the Price Tags? (Thomas Nelson Publishers, 1987)
20 Hot Potatoes Christians Are Afraid to Touch (Word Publishing, 1988)
Growing Up in America: A Sociology of Youth Ministry (Zondervan, 1989)
Things We Wish We Had Said: Reflections of a Father and His Grown Son, with Bart Campolo (Thomas Nelson, 1989)
The Church and the American Teenager (Zondervan, 1989)
Wake Up America! Answering God's Radical Call While Living in the Real World (HarperCollins, 1991)

How to Be Pentecostal without Speaking in Tongues (Word Publishing, 1991)

50 Ways You Can Feed a Hungry World, with Gordon Aeschliman (InterVarsity Press, 1991)

Sociology through the Eyes of Faith, with David A. Fraser (HarperSanFrancisco, 1992)

How to Rescue the Earth without Worshiping Nature: A Christian's Call to Save Creation (Thomas Nelson, 1992)

Everything You've Heard Is Wrong (Word Publishing, 1992)

The Kingdom of God Is a Party: God's Radical Plan for His Family (Word Publishing, 1992)

50 Ways You Can Share Your Faith, with Gordon Aeschliman (InterVarsity Press, 1992)

50 Ways You Can Save the Planet, with Gordon Aeschliman (InterVarsity Press, 1992)

Stand Up and Be Counted: How to Change the World for Good (Zondervan, 1993)

50 Ways You Can Be Pro-Life, with Gordon Aeschliman (InterVarsity Press, 1993)

50 Ways You Can Reach the World, with Gordon Aeschliman (InterVarsity Press, 1993)

101 Ways Your Church Can Change the World, with Gordon Aeschliman (InterVarsity Press, 1993)

Carpe Diem: Seize the Day (Word Publishing, 1994)

Is Jesus a Republican or a Democrat? And 14 Other Polarizing Issues (Thomas Nelson, 1995)

Can Mainline Denominations Make a Comeback? (Judson Press, 1995)

Following Jesus without Embarrassing God (Word Publishing, 1997)

Let Me Tell You a Story: Life Lessons from Unexpected Places and Unlikely People (Thomas Nelson, 2000)

Revolution and Renewal: How Churches Are Saving Our Cities, with Bruce Main (Westminster John Knox Press, 2000)

Which Jesus: Choosing between Love and Power (Thomas Nelson, 2002)

The Survival Guide for Christians on Campus: How to Be Students and Disciples at the Same Time, with William H. Willimon (Howard Books, 2002)

Adventures in Missing the Point: How the Culture-Controlled Church Neutered the Gospel, with Brian D. McLaren (Youth Specialties, 2003)

Speaking My Mind: The Radical Evangelical Prophet Tackles the Tough Issues Christians Are Afraid to Face (Thomas Nelson, 2004)

The Church Enslaved: A Spirituality for Racial Reconciliation, with Michael Battle (Augsburg Fortress Press, 2005)

Letters to a Young Evangelical (Basic Books, 2006)

Everybody Wants to Change the World: Practical Ideas for Social Justice, with Gordon Aeschliman (Regal Books, 2006)

The God of Intimacy and Action: Reconnecting Ancient Spiritual Practices, Evangelism, and Justice, with Mary Darling (Jossey-Bass, 2007)

Red Letter Christians: A Citizen's Guide to Faith and Politics (Regal Books, 2008)

Partly Right: Learning from the Critics of Christianity (Thomas Nelson, 2008)

Stories That Feed Your Soul (Baker Books, 2010)

Connecting like Jesus: Practices for Healing, Teaching, and Preaching, with Mary Darling (Jossey-Bass, 2010)

Choose Love Not Power: How to Right the World's Wrongs from a Place of Weakness (Baker Books, 2009)

Red Letter Revolution: What If Jesus Really Meant What He Said?, with Shane Claiborne (Thomas Nelson, 2012)

Why I Left, Why I Stayed: Conversations on Christianity between an Evangelical Father and His Humanist Son, written with Bart Campolo (HarperCollins, 2018)

Pilgrim: A Theological Memoir, with Steve Rabey (Eerdmans, 2025)

A ninety-seven-page index to topics covered in Tony's books is available here:

https://www.tonycampolo.org/wp-content/uploads/2019/06/Tony-Campolo-Book-Index-by-Topics.pdf

A thirty-two-page index of Scriptures used in Tony's books is available here:

https://www.tonycampolo.org/wp-content/uploads/2019/06/Tony-Campolo-Book-Index-by-Scripture.pdf